or

A Gift for

_____

from

_____

Date

_____

the
GLORY
has
COME

the
GLORY
has
COME

Encountering the Wonder of Christmas

An Advent Devotional

LARRY SPARKS

DESTINY IMAGE® PUBLISHERS, INC.
P.O. Box 310, Shippensburg, PA 17257-0310
"Promoting Inspired Lives."

This book and all other Destiny Image and Destiny Image Fiction books are available at Christian bookstores and distributors worldwide.

Cover design by Christian Rafetto

For more information on foreign distributors, call 717-532-3040.

Reach us on the Internet: www.destinyimage.com.

ISBN 13 HC: 978-0-7684-5090-3
ISBN 13 TP: 978-0-7684-5093-4
ISBN 13 eBook: 978-0-7684-5091-0
ISBN 13 LP: 978-0-7684-5092-7

For Worldwide Distribution, Printed in the U.S.A.

TP 1 2 3 4 5 6 7 8 / 23 22 21 20 19

HC 1 2 3 4 5 6 7 8 / 23 22 21 20 19

CONTENTS

INTRODUCTION

I love Christmas. Everything about the holiday season makes my heart come alive! You name it and it's most likely on my "Top Ten Christmas List." Carols, family get-togethers, Christmas cards, food in abundance, cookies, decorations, wide-eyed wonder, cantatas, food, church programs, the lights, garland, food, etc. Did I mention food? The list goes on. And yet, in the midst of all of our celebration and festivity, it's possible that the true wonder and glory of the season can get lost as we focus on a bunch of "good" things.

Why settle for good when *glory* is available?

God has moved toward us. Glory has come—glory is here. The Incarnation, the Word of God becoming flesh, is the great evidence that we are not waiting for a move of God to come one day, someday. God has already moved toward humanity and Heaven is awaiting a response from the earth. What will we do with His movement? How will we respond? I'm convinced the greatest lessons we could ever learn about welcoming a true move of God are found right here in the often too-familiar story of Christmas.

It is my honor to present to you twenty-five Advent devotions and reflections that will help powerfully connect you with the true Spirit of the Christmas season, *the Holy Spirit.* We commonly recognize that the Spirit of God is the great evangelist and revealer of Jesus. When someone receives Jesus as Lord and Savior, that person has a supernatural encounter with the Holy Spirit, where God Himself brings their dead spirit out of darkness and translates this once-lost soul into the Kingdom of God (see Colossians 1:13).

This same Spirit, I believe, testifies of Jesus the Son, born in a manger. There is revelation wrapped up in those swaddling clothes that, when received and applied, will bring you, individually, and the body of Christ, corporately, into the greatest days of glory, power, and Holy Spirit demonstration the earth has ever seen. For those seeking the "blueprint of revival," look no further than swaddling clothes and a manger.

My prayer is that each of these amazing authors, through the anointing on their unique entries, would spiritually disarm you concerning the Christmas story.

This is not a standard Advent devotional. Each author carries a powerful, prophetic, and Spirit-filled perspective that will perhaps challenge the way you have engaged the Christmas story and season in the past. Good!

I pray that the familiarity and tradition associated with this season would be broken in our lives. I pray that all of us would change our mindsets concerning this amazing holiday. A million yeses to the family, food, and functions of the season—but never at the expense of encountering the glory of the newborn King.

What a joy to go on this journey with you!

—Larry Sparks
Publisher, Destiny Image

GOD MAKES
THE FIRST MOVE

by Larry Sparks

And the Word became flesh and dwelt among us, and we have seen his glory, glory as of the only Son from the Father, full of grace and truth (John 1:14).

e trivialize the Christmas celebration when we reduce it to what's familiar. I'm certainly grateful for everything portrayed in our pageants and nativity scenes. Each element carries profound and powerful revelation, regardless of how many times we see it on a Christmas card or as a statuette outside of a beautiful cathedral. But let's step back for a moment and consider the very purpose of the Christmas season—God moving toward humankind.

The Incarnation, *the Word becoming flesh and dwelling among us,* represents the eternal protocol of Heaven— God moves first, then we move in response to His movement. Otherwise, we are incapable of moving without God moving upon us first.

We only love Him because He first loved us (see 1 John 4:19). We can only draw near to God because God first drew near to us (see James 4:8).

We can only respond to God because while we were dead in our sins and trespasses, God sought us—we didn't seek Him (see Romans 5:8; Ephesians 2:1-4). He stepped into our darkness and flooded it with His redeeming light.

Throughout church history, the great "moves of God" that we often identify as revivals, awakenings, or outpourings of the Holy Spirit were, I believe, the combination of two key elements: the sovereignty of God and the stewardship of humankind. God moved, yes; but I am convinced that the supernatural intensity of revival is the collision of humankind moving toward God.

Often, people are waiting on or praying for a "move of God" when they fail to realize that God has already made the first move.

GOD MOVED TOWARD HUMANKIND

There are three key biblical illustrations that showcase how God has definitively moved toward humankind through the Man and Messiah, Christ Jesus: the Incarnation, the torn veil, and the day of Pentecost.

The Incarnation

*So **the Word** became human and **made his home among us**. He was full of unfailing love and faithfulness. And we have seen his glory, the glory of the Father's one and only Son* (John 1:14 NLT).

During Christmastime, we celebrate the ultimate move of God—the Word condescending from Heaven, taking upon Himself frail humanity, and serving as the Messiah-Man who was 100 percent God and 100 percent Man. God came from Heaven to earth to live a perfect life, die a perfect death, and then rise from the dead, granting humanity access to God in three realms.

Through the perfect life of Jesus, we receive sanctification because it's no longer us who live, but Christ in us (see Galatians 2:20). It's faith in His perfect life that is key for our sanctifying process—the journey of becoming more and more like Jesus while we walk this planet. It's faith in His perfect death that redeems us spiritually.

By placing our faith in His perfect atoning work, our spiritual status changes. We are delivered out of the kingdom of darkness and translated into His Kingdom as sons and daughters of God (see Colossians 1:13). Finally, it's faith in His resurrection which affirms that one day, we too will share completely in His resurrected glory by also having glorified bodies (Romans 6:5; Philippians 3:20-21).

The Torn Veil

*Jesus passionately cried out, took his last breath, and gave up his spirit. At that moment **the veil in the Holy of Holies was torn in two from the top to the bottom**...* (Matthew 27:50-51 TPT).

One of the key cataclysmic moments during the death of Jesus was the tearing of the temple veil from top to the bottom. It was though the invisible hand of the Lord tore apart this exceedingly thick fabric, proclaiming that a physical building would no longer restrain or contain the presence of God. Now all who would receive the Messiah's atoning work on the Cross would become the *temple of God,* for His Spirit would take up residence within them (see 1 Corinthians 6:19).

After all, it was the Lord who asked David through the prophet Nathan: *"Thus says the Lord: Would you build me a house to dwell in?"* (2 Samuel 7:5). Later we see the Lord ask a similar question: *"Thus says the Lord: 'Heaven is my throne, and the earth is my footstool; what is the house that you would build for me, and what is the place of my rest?'"* (Isaiah 66:1). God had long sought a resting place on earth, but not one created by human hands—one that He Himself had fashioned. This resting place would become redeemed humanity. If Jesus shed His blood to make atonement for our sins and grant us passage to eternal life in Heaven, that would have been beyond sufficient.

However, the Old Covenant pointed to another dimension. The Scriptures of old spoke little of Heaven, although that is definitely a tremendous benefit and blessing of being redeemed. Rather, the Old Covenant pointed to a day when the barrier of sin was removed so that humankind could become the new resting place for the Spirit of God.

> *I will sprinkle clean water on you, and you shall be clean from all your uncleannesses, and from all your idols I will cleanse you. And I will give you a new heart, and a new spirit I will put within you. And I will remove the heart of stone from your flesh and give you a heart of flesh. And I will put my Spirit within you, and cause you to walk in my statutes and be careful to obey my rules* (Ezekiel 36:25-27).

The Day of Pentecost

> *On the day of Pentecost* **all the believers were meeting together in one place. Suddenly,** *there was a sound from heaven like the roaring of a mighty windstorm, and it filled the house where they were sitting* (Acts 2:1-2 NLT).

The Old Testament prophecies that spoke of the Holy Spirit came to a dramatic fulfillment on the Day of Pentecost. God's home address had changed—at least partially. No more Ark of the Covenant. No more tents or tabernacles. The Spirit of God officially moved out, changed locations, and now, because the work of redemption had been performed and the sins of human-kind had been absorbed by the spotless Lamb, it was possible for sinful flesh to actually become a house for the Holy God. The Son of God ascended to the right hand of God the Father.

And yet, prior to leaving His disciples, Jesus made a promise that He would not leave them alone as orphans (see John 14:18). He promised to send the Comforter, the Helper, the one called the Holy Spirit. We are not waiting for another Pentecost. Only One Man will one day split the sky and return to planet Earth—Jesus. Until then, we are not waiting on another outpouring to come from above; if anything, Heaven is waiting for this outpouring to come out of the temple and flow into the Earth, bringing healing, salvation, and transformation to the nations. Where is this temple? It's you and it's me.

To summarize, God has made the definitive move toward humanity. We see this beginning with the Incarnation, continuing with the torn veil and then culminating with the Day of Pentecost. God made the first move; how will we respond?

What Is Our Response to the Move of God?

In studying the great revivals that have punctuated the past two thousand years of church history, I've discovered a common denominator that seems nonnegotiable to catalyzing a powerful outpouring of the Spirit—*the people's determination to move toward God*. The following are but a few examples:

We see evangelist George Whitefield and Methodist pioneer John Wesley persisting in prayer until the power of God fell upon them.

Charles Finney was frustrated over the lack of effectiveness in people's prayers. This frustration fueled his hunger and thirst to experience God at any cost. As a result, on October 10, 1821, he experienced a powerful filling by the Holy Spirit. He urged the people to pray to God earnestly and expectantly for the immediate outpouring of the Spirit.

Phoebe Palmer opened her home for what became known as the "Tuesday meeting," making space for people to come and experience the deeper Christian life through a touch by the Spirit.

Jeremiah Lamphier was a businessman in New York City who felt led to start a noontime weekly prayer meeting. He was willing to persist after the first few meetings were received by poor attendance. As a result, he pioneered a great prayer revival that undoubtedly was responsible for birthing some of the most demonstrative and historical revival movements that would come in the decades to follow.

Andrew Murray longed and prayed for revival in South Africa. His desperation for God to move with power and demonstration is palpable when reading his various Spirit-filled works.

Dwight L. Moody became desperate and thirsty for God, crying out for a baptism in the Spirit. His cry for this filling was consistent and persistent. Following Moody's power encounter with God, it is said that even though he didn't radically alter his evangelistic methods, the fruitfulness of his ministry shifted significantly and many more people received Christ because of his outreach.

In Wales, Evan Roberts began to hunger and thirst for God as a thirteen-year-old boy. He had two requests of the Lord: 1) for God to fill him with the Holy Spirit; and 2) for God to send revival to Wales. History books record that both requests were fulfilled, as Roberts was the key catalyst and noteworthy personality attached to the 1904 Welsh Revival.

Frank Bartleman was an intercessor who contended for a historic outpouring of the Holy Spirit in the United States. William Seymour was a half-blind African American minister living in a very racially hostile era. Who would have thought that Bartleman's travailing intercession combined with Seymour's bold hunger for Holy Spirit baptism would have produced the Azusa

Street Revival of 1906, birthing the modern Pentecostal movement.

From the 1900s onward, there are multiple examples—some local and some global—of men, women, and entire church communities who moved toward God in the place of prayer, desperation, and hunger. Not only did they cry out in the place of prayer, but they were willing to make room for God to move in the ways He saw fit. That was huge.

Who will make room for the move of God? Mary and Joseph did. In the lowliest of conditions, they accommodated the prophesied plan of God.

Will We Embrace His Move?

It's one thing to claim to want God; it's another thing entirely to accept His move on His terms. He often comes in ways that we don't expect to offend our minds while drawing us into a place of intimate communion with Him. It's always God's friends who recognize Him first. The way He moves might seem dramatically different from the anticipated or expected, but those who are His intimates will always see His steadfast face through the often-unusual works of His hand.

These friends can see the joy of the Lord through what appears to be uproarious, uncontrollable laughter. They can see the power of the Lord through what appears to be people falling down, "slain in the Spirit." They can see the wonder of the Lord through unusual signs and manifestations of His presence. They can see the freedom of the Lord when someone is delivered of demonic oppression or possession. They will see the awe of the Lord when someone shakes or trembles in His presence.

These are some common "manifestations" that take place during seasons of revival. They are only controversial because we think they are new, or somehow contrary to the personality of God. They are neither. They challenge us because they demonstrate that the God we read about is actually real. He's not a baby in a manger anymore, nor is He a broken man on a cross.

Yes, He was born into the earth as a babe wrapped in swaddling clothes, and we know that He died a criminal's death on a Roman cross for the sins of the world, but the story did not end there—and we should not live, think, or function like it did. Jesus rose from the grave, ascended to Heaven, and prayed that the Father would send another Helper to earth who would be the Spirit of Christ dwelling in our midst.

He's alive! He moves. He touches. He heals. His presence has a measurable, tangible impact on the environment around us.

God moved toward humankind, so that we might move toward God. End result? A move of God through moving people.

PRAYER

Lord, draw me close to You. I want to be Your friend. I don't seek You because of the benefits or blessing—You are my great reward. I want to know You so deeply that even when You move in ways that might seem new or different, I will recognize it's You because I'll see Your face. I'll see Your nature and character being revealed and unveiled. Help me to be like the shepherds and wise men who were not offended by Jesus.

LARRY SPARKS is publisher for Destiny Image, a Spirit-filled publishing house birthed in 1983 with a mandate to publish the prophets. With a MDiv. in Church History and Renewal from Regent University, Larry is a prophetic minister who teaches individuals and church environments how to create space for the Holy Spirit to move in presence, prophetic utterance and power. Larry has been featured on Sid Roth's *It's Supernatural!*, *The Jim Bakker Show*, CBN, TBN, the Elijahlist, and *Charisma* magazine. Larry is also host of *The Prophetic Edge* featured on GOD TV. He lives in Texas with his wife and daughter. For more information visit: larrysparksministries.com.

HOW TO RESPOND TO A GOD ENCOUNTER

by Heidi Baker

This is the story of two people in the Bible who each had a powerful encounter with God; however, they responded in two very different ways. We all want to have an encounter; and when He comes, it is our privilege to respond with our yes. I wish I could say that it is easier after we receive a promise from God and that everything just falls into place. That may not be the case. When we truly have an encounter, by His grace we can carry whatever He gives us to full term no matter what it costs—but there is a cost.

In Luke 1:5, we read about a priest named Zechariah and his wife, Elizabeth. The Bible says they were living blamelessly, following the commands of God. What would that be like to follow God perfectly? They were living blamelessly, *but*.... Some of us have many "buts," when we just want the promise. *But* Zechariah and Elizabeth had no children because Elizabeth was barren, and they were already older. Then, Zechariah was chosen by random to go into the temple and burn incense. The others were worshipping outside.

Not everyone was allowed to go into the holy place. It is a privilege that we are free to gather and worship God. The blood of Jesus made a way for us to enter in, but some people do not value this privilege. Don't stay outside when He paid a great price to be face to face with you. I love leading people to Jesus and seeing orphans coming home to the Father's house, but my greatest joy is being face to face with the One who is worthy. All of my motivation comes from that place of worship.

Zechariah was in this amazing place of encounter when the angel appeared to him. Can you imagine? It is funny how the angels often say, "Don't be afraid." Yeah right. If there was a big angel in your room, you would be afraid.

> *But the angel said to him, "Do not be afraid, Zechariah, for your prayer has been heard, and your wife Elizabeth will bear you a son, and you shall call his name John. And you will have joy and gladness, and many will*

rejoice at his birth, for he will be great before the Lord…" (Luke 1:13-15).

What is your prayer? I want you to think about it. You may just want enough money to pay your rent. That's okay, you need to have somewhere to sleep. But when you are deeply connected to Jesus, you are going to start to pray very bold prayers. My prayer was: "I want a nation! I want to see millions of people come to You, Jesus. I want the unreached people groups to come to You, Jesus!" My prayers started to grow. I was no longer just praying for my family or my basic needs, but prayers like: "God, I want a nation. I want to see people worshipping You all over the planet, no matter what it takes."

When I had a seven-day encounter with God, I felt like I was being electrocuted and screamed out, "I'm going to die!" I sensed God responding, "Good, I want you dead." He doesn't leave you dead, but He lets you feel the dying. Allow Him to work on you during those times of encounter. You need to totally and completely die, and there is something fearful about that.

God is a good, loving Father, but you have to die to your own ambition and the things that hinder you from living a life fully yielded to Him. Then He can resurrect you. During my encounter, I didn't know if I would ever walk or talk again, but I kept seeing waves of the love of Jesus. All I could do was worship. Even though I couldn't speak, I worshipped in silence with tears running down my face.

Zechariah's prayer was for fruitfulness. He wanted a child, but he gave up on his dream. The angel of the Lord came even though he no longer believed. He spoke about John's incredible calling. What a promise! God wants to put His promises in you. Every human being who is a lover of Jesus is meant to live face to face with the Lamb. If you live face to face, you are going to be fruitful! Sometimes there will be pruning; but if you keep abiding, the fruit will come. Even the cutting away and discipline of the Lord is so you will bear much fruit.

You already may have had incredible promises from God. You may be seeing them come to pass. Or you may be walking a life of silence, muted and deaf from your unbelief. We want an encounter. We want God to speak to us. We want God to send His holy fire and burn up all our flesh and cause us to be fully filled, but what do we do when the promise is prophesied? What do we do when God speaks to us?

Zechariah had a beautiful promise answered by the Lord Himself through the messenger Gabriel. You would think he would be joyful, hopeful, and full of faith because God heard his prayer. Instead, Zechariah questions the angel how this is possible since he is old. He followed the commands of God, he was picked at random, he was on his face worshipping, and an angel showed up! How could he not believe? But in that moment, he doubted, thinking about his physical circumstances.

The angel said, *"I am Gabriel. I stand in the presence of God, and I was sent to speak to you and to bring you this good news. And behold, you will be silent and unable to speak until the day that these things take place, because you did not believe my words, which will be fulfilled in their time"* (Luke 1:19-20). Our promises will still be fulfilled even if we don't believe because God knows what He is doing, and He promised what He promised. Zechariah would have a son even though he did not believe, but because of his unbelief, he was silenced.

There is another way of responding to God, the way of faith. A way that says yes even when challenges come against us. A way that says yes, no matter what it costs. Any mother who has given birth understands that it is costly, and it can be very painful. It can be very difficult. At times our promises take so long that we struggle to keep believing, but we have to keep crying yes!

When we read the story of Mary, many of us think of the Christmas nativity plays at church. In Mozambique, we just grab a baby "Jesus" out of the baby house. We have plenty of children to act out the story. We tie goats to a rope bed. I love it. Especially because in our province, there was no word in the Makua dialect for Christmas because they were all people of another faith, now there are thousands of churches and houses of prayer. I love Christmas when it is holy and pure and focused on the One who is worthy, Jesus. But real angels are not like cute children wearing white sheets.

The same angel that was sent to Zechariah came to Mary and said, *"Greetings, O favored one, the Lord is with you!"* (Luke 1:28). Do you want favor? We say we want the favor of God, but what does favor look like? Sometimes favor looks like something you are not expecting. Sometimes people will be shaking their finger concerning your favor. What is a teenage Jewish virgin going to do with this kind of favor? And what is her response going to be? Is her response going to be like Zechariah trying to be quiet and cover up her favor? There is only so long you can do that.

Mary is there in the presence of God. I always imagined her frying fish or washing her clothes in a clay bucket. She had the same initial response—she was greatly troubled. The angel said, *"Don't be afraid."* Then he goes on to tell her what the favor looks like:

> *And behold, you will conceive in your womb and bear a son, and you shall call his name Jesus. He will be great and will be called the Son of the Most High. And the Lord God will give to him the throne of his father David, and he will reign over the house of Jacob forever, and of his kingdom, there will be no end* (Luke 1:31-33).

Wow, that is favor. Nobody on this planet will ever again have the privilege that Mary had. There is only one Jesus, fully God and fully man, born to a virgin. But all of us can carry the promises of God that He put inside us.

Are you ready? What will your response be? One response is feeling like it is just too much, and you don't really believe, and you are silenced. God will still do what He said He would do. He is sovereign. You may think that because of God's sovereignty it doesn't matter what you do. Will you participate? Will you carry glory? Will you allow God to use your little life? Will you give birth to what God put inside you?

Zechariah returned home and Elizabeth became pregnant. She was probably scared to believe it, but as that child began to grow within her womb, her joy started to rise. Perhaps you are thirty years pregnant; but if you do not abort, if you do not miscarry, your promise will come to pass in Jesus' name.

There are promises I received twenty-three years ago that I am still waiting for. Mercifully I have also seen God fulfill a whole lot on the way. Fourteen years ago, He said to build a university. We have buildings ready for three majors, we just need the final documents from the government. These precious ones who live in mud huts, in the villages, will become the leaders of the nation for the glory of God. I just believe.

Whatever God puts in you, believe. Will there be a massive yes cry within you concerning the promises of God? Or will you succumb to a muted life like Zechariah when God encounters you?

When Mary had her heavenly encounter, she too wondered, how will this be? Stating the fact that she was a virgin (Luke 1:34). The angel said that the Holy Spirit would come upon her. We need to position our hearts for the Holy Spirit to come upon us. We are all in different seasons: you may feel dry or full of the oil of the Spirit; you may be longing for more, to be overshadowed by God; maybe you are in a place of fear where you have been silenced. Whatever space you are in, you can ask Him to come—then position yourself for the overshadowing of the Lord as you worship and adore Him.

Mary responded, *"Behold, I am the servant of the Lord; let it be to me according to your word"* (Luke 1:38). Will you respond like Zechariah or like Mary to the promises of God?

PRAYER AND REFLECTION

As the Lord's yielded servants, let's pray Mary's anointed prayer: "I am Your servant, Lord; may it be to me according to Your word."

Think of the promises of God in your life. Think of the times God has overshadowed you. Cry out like Mary. The angel tells Mary that nothing will be impossible with God. None of the things He promises you are impossible, no matter what your circumstances look like. Nothing is impossible with God. Choose to believe. Then when it gets hard, choose to keep believing. Let your life be worship, and let your only cry be "Yes!"

HEIDI BAKER founded Iris Ministries with her husband, Rolland. Together they served as missionaries in Indonesia, Hong Kong, and the streets of London before following God's calling in 1995 to Mozambique. Having faced overwhelming need, the Bakers now watch God provide miraculously for over 7,000 children. Heidi is the author of *Compelled by Love* and *Birthing the Miraculous* and coauthor with her husband of *Always Enough* and *Expecting Miracles*.

CHRISTMAS: A SEASON OF FAMILY, GIVING, AND JOY

by Bill Johnson

ne of my favorite songs sung during the Christmas season is "Joy to the World." It is a song of profound intercession, the meaning of which sometimes gets lost through familiarity. The line, "Let earth receive her King," is one of the most important prayers ever prayed. It's a cry: Let the people of this planet receive Jesus as their king.

The Scripture says, *"As many as received Him, to them He gave the right to become children of God…"* (John 1:12

NKJV). It is a cry for ongoing, continuous revival for the nations as people receive Jesus as their Lord, their Savior, their King.

The song continues with, "Let every heart prepare Him room. Let Heaven and nature sing...." When people yield to the Lord Jesus Christ in salvation, they are taking the first step into His eternal purpose, which is found in the wonderful reality of earth being influenced by Heaven. Jesus taught them the nature of His will when He taught them to pray, *"Your will be done, on earth as it is in heaven"* (Matthew 6:10).

It's in the Christmas story where God first reveals this part of His plan saying, *"Glory to God in the highest, and on earth peace among those with whom he is pleased!"* (Luke 2:14). The glory in His world is to have an effect on the reality of this one. This is where God begins to unfold His plan that Heaven comes to earth.

Within the reality of God's reign in Heaven, existing without any hindrance from the distorted will of people, is the model of what He purposes to do here on earth. Heaven is to affect earth.

Interestingly, when it comes to the conversion of souls, earth inspires Heaven, as all the angels in Heaven rejoice when someone is saved.

As people surrender to Jesus, they inspire elaborate joy in Heaven. All of Heaven rejoices because people come to Christ here on earth. That is the strategy the Lord put into place. Christmas is to forever create in our minds the picture of the perfect cooperation between Heaven and earth, and between earth and Heaven.

RESPONSIBILITY AND JOY

Jesus taught His disciples about the mysterious access to ever-increasing joy in the parable of the talents. A talent was a sum of money. Three servants were given different amounts of wealth to steward and grow for their master. Two of the servants invested the money wisely and returned the talents with increase. The master, having seen their wisdom, praised them, telling them that he will increase their responsibility because they have proven to be faithful: *"...You have been faithful and trustworthy over a little, I will put you in charge of many things; share in the joy of your master"* (Matthew 25:21 Amplified Bible).

Is the increase of responsibility and the entrance into His joy two separate rewards? I don't think so. I believe it's more appropriate to say these are two sides of the same coin. We were designed to co-labor with God, which is key to a healthy identity. And it is in this identity that we exhibit the lifestyle of joy. Perhaps the greatest example of this principle is when Jesus told His disciples that they could ask for whatever they wanted—prayer is co-laboring—and the Father would give it to them. He concluded His point with the statement that these answers to prayer would come *"that your joy may be full"* (John 16:24 NKJV).

Both servants are rewarded for their wise stewardship, and the reward was increased responsibility and
joy. The master didn't just tell them to be joyful. He told
them to enter into *His* joy (Matthew 25:21 NKJV). Jesus
has more joy than anyone. *"…God has anointed You with
the oil of gladness above Your companions"* (Hebrews 1:9
Amplified Bible). "Gladness" here is exuberant joy! We
do not have a distant, uncaring God. It's quite the opposite. He is moved by whatever moves us. When He invites
us into a lifestyle of joy, He is not commanding us to do
something that is separate from who He is. He is inviting
us into His prosperous heart. It's His joy.

It would be easy to make a strong theological case
for developing many different qualities found in the
nature and character of Christ. We know the importance
of faith, for *"without faith it is impossible to please Him"*
(Hebrews 11:6). We know that there is faith, hope, and
that, *"the greatest of these is love"* (1 Corinthians 13:13). I
could go through a great list of vital attributes of God.
But I have a sense that peace and joy are the things that
will stop your neighbors in their tracks, as they illustrate
the reality of the Kingdom of God so beautifully (Romans
14:17). There is a wonderful connection between these
two realities.

For me, joy is peace out loud; peace is quiet joy. The
world is hungry to know what true joy looks like. And
there is nothing else in creation designed to model this
joy in the measure of Christ Himself, *except you and me.*

Violent and Excessive Joy

Some think that the wise men were royalty, kings of a faraway land. Others say they were astrologers, studying the stars. Regardless, there is little doubt that they would have been known as the intelligentsia of their day. With an extensive understanding of astronomy, this group of highly educated leaders set out on a journey to find the Messiah. For nearly two years, they traveled. They searched through foreign lands to find the One to whom the star was pointing.

The magi came to see a King who could do nothing for them. Unlike the Queen of Sheba, who came to King Solomon that he might explain great mysteries, or give her insights to solve life's greatest problems. This was different. These wise men journeyed for years to find a baby who was born the King. And they did it all for the sake of worship. They came to worship Jesus for who He was, not for what He could do.

Before they found the Messiah, they met with King Herod. After their meeting the Bible says:

*They went on their way. And behold, the star that they had seen when it rose went before them until it came to rest over the place where the child was. When they saw the star, they **rejoiced exceedingly with great joy*** (Matthew 2:9-10).

When the wise men saw the star, when they realized that the very thing they had been yearning for was coming to pass, they *rejoiced exceedingly with great joy.* "Exceedingly" has two basic definitions: excessively and violently. That doesn't quite paint the usual picture we have of these studious, regal men who approached the King bearing gifts. But the Bible says their joy was violent and excessive.

Joy is an unexplainable weapon. It is not something we arrive at through logic and reason, at least not the reasoning of this world. The psalmist instructs us to *"rejoice with trembling"* in Psalm 2:11. This passage helps us to see that there is a connection between joy and the fear of God. And we know that when we delight in God, the powers of darkness are terrified. But in this Scripture about the wise men, their joy is extreme.

Valuing Extremes

When the woman poured out the bottle of expensive ointment on Jesus, every one of the crowd thought it was excessive (see Matthew 26:6-13). That money could have been saved and given to the poor. But the woman had come to worship Jesus, and the fragrance of that filled the house. None of the other expressions of worship in that room were written about in the Bible. Her story, though, will be spoken of forever. Maybe it's time to be known for our excessive worship of Jesus our Savior.

The magi rejoiced without restraint when they realized that they were about to see Jesus. This is what their worship looked like. Joy, with a violent effect on the powers of darkness. It's as if, while we're worshipping and enjoying His presence, Jesus goes out and thrashes the enemy, and then returns calling us mighty warriors. And all we did was delight in Him. Is this not the point of Isaiah 42:13? *"The Lord goes out like a mighty man, like a man of war...."*

The enemy loves to turn us inward—searching for answers within ourselves—because there is no source of joy or life there. If he can get my focus off of Jesus and, instead, get me to start self-evaluating, the end result is always negative. But when I consider the Lord, I get to access the very source of joy and peace. I get to realign myself with the lifestyle of joy.

You and I were designed to recognize Him, to be a unique sound and a unique pleasure to Him. We were designed as instruments of joy and peace.

UNDERSTANDING BRINGS CELEBRATION

Before Nehemiah rebuilt the walls of Jerusalem, the people had been living outside of the protection and covering of the Lord for one hundred fifty years. When the walls were completed, and the city was beginning to repopulate, the prophet Ezra read the Scripture to the people. Gathered in crowds around him, men and women stood together to hear the Law of Moses read for the first time in their lives. Hearing it, they realized how far they had fallen short of God's original plan.

And they began to weep.

This would be a totally appropriate response to conviction in most churches. But Nehemiah puts a stop to it. He says:

> *This day is holy to the Lord your God; do not mourn or weep. …Go your way. Eat the fat and drink sweet wine and send portions to anyone who has nothing ready, for this day is holy to our Lord. And do not be grieved, for **the joy of the Lord is your strength*** (Nehemiah 8:9-10).

They were to offer a much costlier offering than mourning over sin could ever express. They were to rejoice before they had earned it. This kind of offering would take much greater faith.

The entire community had just realized for the first time that they have been living outside of God's plan for their lives, and Nehemiah told them to quit crying and to celebrate. Those are easy words to read on a page, but to have someone command you to be joyful when you are in the midst of repentance is almost insulting.

Naturally, we think, *Let me work my way out of this righteous sorrow and then maybe in three days I can feel a little joy.* But Nehemiah is telling them to be joyful now. It's obvious that they didn't feel like it, but the joy he is talking about is not that kind of joy. The joy of the Lord is sometimes the kind of joy you get when you rejoice.

In the world, you rejoice when you're joyful; but in the Kingdom, you get joyful by rejoicing. Nehemiah tells them to stop mourning, to enter into the joy of the Lord, and the Bible says that, *"All the people went their way to eat and drink and to send portions and to make great rejoicing, because they had understood the words that were declared to them"* (Nehemiah 8:12). They began to celebrate because they understood.

The moment you understand who God is—the moment the divine nature is planted in you—joy is the only appropriate response.

The wise men had traveled far to honor the King of kings with their treasures. When they saw the star that they had been following stopped over where Jesus was, when they understood that the Messiah had been born and that they would see Him, they *"rejoiced exceedingly with great joy."* This is the Christmas story—the Good News. That God Himself came to earth to represent His will for all eternity: let it be on earth as it is in Heaven. The joy of the Father is our inheritance, here and now. And it only gets better.

As Isaiah prophesied, *"There will be no end to the increase of His government or of peace…"* (Isaiah 9:7 NASB). There has never been a moment, since Isaiah spoke these words, that the Kingdom has been in retreat. There has never been loss. It has never been "three steps forward and two steps backward." The Kingdom is always advancing, regardless of our circumstances.

Jesus was born in a manger. He's not that picky where He shows up. In actuality, He is attracted to brokenness and messes. There is no end to the presence of His grace that overrides every circumstance. There is no end to His joy and His peace. There is no end to His government.

Merry Christmas! This is the simple Gospel.

PRAYER

Dear heavenly Father, we rejoice without restraint when we realize that we can see our Lord and Savior Jesus Christ whenever we worship in His name. Like the magi, when we worship, our joy has a violent effect on the powers of darkness. Thank You that while we worship and enjoy His presence, He goes out and thrashes the enemy who means us harm.

BILL JOHNSON is a fifth-generation pastor with a rich heritage in the Holy Spirit. Bill and his wife, Beni, are the senior leaders of Bethel Church in Redding, California, and serve a growing number of churches that cross denominational lines, demonstrate power, and partner for revival. Bill's vision is for all believers to experience God's presence and operate in the miraculous—as expressed in his best-selling books, *When Heaven Invades Earth* and *Hosting the Presence*. The Johnsons have three children and ten grandchildren.

MAKE ROOM FOR THE WONDER

by Lana Vawser

For God so loved the world that He gave His only begotten Son, that whoever believes in Him should not perish but have everlasting life (John 3:16 NKJV).

I sit here with my favorite tea in my favorite tea cup watching the flame of a candle flickering away and my heart is filled with wonder as I ponder the birth of Jesus. When we take a moment to truly stop and think about this life-changing, transforming truth that John 3:16 encompasses, that powerful truth reveals incredible love for humankind that began in a stable.

The Son of God, fully God and fully man, a supernatural conception by the Holy Spirit, birthed through

His mother Mary to come to earth to restore eternal salvation, forgiveness of sin, and relationship between God and humankind. Our beautiful Jesus, born in a manger.

As I have pondered the Christmas story over the last year, there was one line in the story that I could not move past.

> And she gave birth to her firstborn son and wrapped him in swaddling cloths and laid him in a manger, because **there was no place for them** in the inn (Luke 2:7).

> When they arrived in Bethlehem, Mary went into labor, and there she gave birth to her firstborn son. After wrapping the newborn baby in strips of cloth, they laid him in a feeding trough since **there was no available space** in any upper room in the village (Luke 2:7 TPT).

Those words, *"There was no place for them"*—I was surprised by the cry that came out of my heart as I read those words: "God, in everything I do, in every area of my life, I want to make room for You. I never want to be in a place where there is a move of Your Spirit and I have not cultivated my life in a way that makes room for You."

Our God is the God of the unexpected. Imagine being one of the shepherds in the field in Luke 2:8-12 (TPT):

> *That night, in a field near Bethlehem, there were shepherds watching over their flocks. **Suddenly,** an*

*angel of the Lord appeared in radiant splendor before them, lighting up the field with the blazing glory of God, and the shepherds were **terrified!** But **the angel reassured them**, saying, "Don't be afraid. For I have come to bring you good news, the most joyous news the world has ever heard! And it is for everyone everywhere! For today in Bethlehem rescuer was born for you. He is the Lord Yahweh, the Messiah, You will recognize him by this miracle sign: You will find a baby wrapped in strips of cloth and lying in a feeding trough!"*

The God of the *suddenly!* Suddenly an angel appeared in radiant splendor and the shepherds were *terrified,* but out of his mouth comes the greatest proclamation the world has ever heard, *"Don't be afraid, for I have come to bring you good news, the most joyous news the world has ever heard!"* The Messiah has been born!

Would those shepherds have been anticipating in their usual nightly routine of tending sheep, that an angel from Heaven would show up and decree the greatest good news the world has ever heard? I doubt it! But in that moment, Heaven invaded earth. In that moment, the supernatural manifested into the natural realm that would leave them and the entire world forever changed.

Imagine the wonder they would have felt looking into the eyes of that angel who was blazing with the glory of the Lord. Imagine the wonder when they found baby Jesus in the stable and they *knew* He was the Messiah, witnessing the Rescuer born for them. Those shepherds would have walked away from that encounter with that angel and went straight-away to find the baby. Staring into the face of baby Jesus, they undoubtedly remained forever changed. Marked for life. Transformed.

It fills my heart with wonder and my eyes with tears as I ponder the privilege it was for those shepherds to be invited in that time of history into witness the greatest demonstration of God's power and His hand of mercy that the world had ever seen.

The wonder that fills my heart, the awe that bubbles up inside me as I reflect on the life-changing truth that Almighty God humbled Himself and came to earth as a baby for me, for you. It births a cry in me and a hunger to know Him, to lay my life down again, a fresh surrender to Him that He would use my life in any way He chooses to extend His Kingdom and see the Good News of the Gospel spread around the earth—that the whole world would be filled with the knowledge of the glory and goodness of God (Habakkuk 2:14 NKJV). That my little life would be used to lift the name of Jesus high and see multitudes come to know His love and saving grace.

But what if He shows up in a way I don't expect? What if He moves in a way that "breaks boxes"? What if His ways are completely different from mine? Am I someone who lives in the position of Second Chronicles 16:9 (NLT)? *"The eyes of the Lord search the whole earth in order to strengthen those whose hearts are fully committed to him...."*

So overwhelmed by His love and the hope of the world that was manifested in the birth of Jesus Christ, that when He grew to be a man, who then died in my place, paid for my sin, and bridged the gap between God and humankind so I could have everlasting life and know Him intimately and walk in everything that is mine in Christ, so undone by these truths, my heart responds with "God, my life is fully Yours. My heart is completely Yours. I yield to You, to Your ways. Teach me to be someone who discerns the move of Your hand in the unexpected ways You move. Teach me to be someone who knows Your ways. May You find room in my life to display Your glory and see Your Kingdom extended and Jesus receive His full reward."

My heart overflows with love for Him and what He did for me—for you!

That's my prayer for you today, friend. That you would hear His heart of love in the Christmas story. That you would be left in wonder and awe again of the radical, never-ending, relentless, unconditional love of God that He came to earth as a baby—for you and for the world.

INVITATION

May you continue to "make room" for Him in your life. May you continue to live your life yielded to His ways, inviting Him to move in however and whatever way He chooses because you want Him above all else, because in those "unexpected ways" He moves are the places where you and I are filled with awe and wonder of who He is and just how majestic He is. May we be people who have eyes to see and ears to hear. There's a whole new world of wonder upon you!

LANA VAWSER is first and foremost, a pursuer of God's heart; and second, a prophetic voice to the nations. Her desire is to help people develop deep intimacy with Jesus and activate their prophetic hearing to recognize God speaking in everyday life. Lana is driven by a vision to see people set free to walk in the abundant life that Jesus purchased for them. She is an itinerant preacher and prophetic revivalist who participates in powerful moves of God throughout the nations. Lana is married to Kevin and they live in Queensland, Australia, with their three sons.

WE SAY "YES" TO
THE MOVE OF GOD!

by Larry Sparks

*And Mary said, "Behold, I am the servant of the
Lord; let it be to me according to your word…"*
(Luke 1:38).

Mary set a timeless example for how we need to respond to God's movement in our lives. We say, "Yes!"

The angel Gabriel gave her a history-shaping assignment, one that her teenage mind surely could not comfortably wrap itself around. And yet, her response was one of obedience. She was willing to serve the word of the Lord.

Mary is a standout figure in the canon of Scripture, being the unique vessel whom Heaven chose to host the Savior of the world in her womb, and I believe there are principles we can learn from how she cooperated with Heaven.

CARRYING THE GLORY

Many people want to experience God's glorious presence, and rightly so! We want to carry and host His presence with our lives. We want to be like the early church, who walked in unusual, supernatural demonstration and power. The Gospel was not just expressed through articulate speech or presentation, but a visible manifestation of the Holy Spirit with power, signs, wonders, and miracles accompanying the Word (see Mark 16:20; 1 Corinthians 2:4, 4:20). We want this, yes, but we often fail to consider what was required of the early church to walk in that measure of power.

It's not perfection God is looking for. It's not fullness of knowledge. It's not even the ability to fully wrap your mind around what He is calling you to do; it's a yielded life that says, "Yes, Lord—on Your terms, not mine!" This was the response of Mary and, I believe, this is what made her life compatible with the greatest assignment in human history, to give birth to Messiah Jesus.

No, you are not giving birth to Jesus like Mary did. But allow me to suggest, for a moment, that Jesus is being revealed in and through your life! God's presence no longer resides in temples or tents or golden boxes. The Babe in the manger grew to become the Man on the Cross and because of that transaction, glory could now dwell amid and within humankind once more.

Those who receive the redemptive work of the Messiah become indwelt by glory through the Person of the Holy Spirit. As a result, the Spirit of God now dwells in the midst of humanity, once again. He lives within us, yes, but I believe He desires to overshadow us and rest upon us with power. As Pastor Bill Johnson has said, "He lives within you for your sake, He rests upon you for the sake of others."

Could it be that Mary could serve as an example to us today of how we can be a compatible "resting place" for the move of God? I think so.

SERVING THE WORD

Consider Mary's response to the angel, *"Behold, I am the servant of the Lord; let it be to me according to your word"* (Luke 1:38).

Often times, our preference would be for the word of the Lord to serve us rather than us serve His word. We want information and clarity first. We want to be able to comfortably understand all the ins and outs of what God is asking us to do. But when God is on the move, He is seeking a people who will move with the flow of His Spirit, regardless of whether or not it makes sense to our natural minds. After all, we are serving and following a supernatural God. It's not that God doesn't outline what He is doing; He often does. The truth is, what He is doing confronts and confounds the way we think. It doesn't often make sense.

Gabriel certainly provided a good deal of information to Mary about Heaven's plan and agenda working through her, explaining:

> *Do not be afraid, Mary, for you have found favor with God. And behold, you will conceive in your womb and bear a son, and you shall call his name Jesus. He will be great and will be called the Son of the Most High. And the Lord God will give to him the throne of his father David, and he will reign over the house of Jacob forever, and of his kingdom there will be no end* (Luke 1:30-33).

This was Mary's assignment. Upon Gabriel's first announcement, we see that Mary *"was greatly troubled at the saying, and tried to discern what sort of greeting this might be"* (Luke 1:29). Her mind was trying to make sense of a supernatural encounter, when in fact, the natural human mind will always fail to fully grasp what's taking place in those sacred moments when Heaven and earth collide.

It doesn't mean we abandon all reason and logic to blindly accept what is happening. Certainly not! But when we know God is summoning us, we need to allow what He is doing and saying to shape the way we think instead of trying to bring God down to our level. He is constantly calling us heavenward, upward, higher. He is ever pressing against the way we think, inviting us to think like He does. Remember how the Lord said through the prophet Isaiah:

For my thoughts are not your thoughts, neither are your ways my ways, declares the Lord. For as the heavens are higher than the earth, so are my ways higher than your ways and my thoughts than your thoughts (Isaiah 55:8-9).

This is what is taking place here in the exchange between Mary and Gabriel. At first, she is troubled by the angelic visitation and tries to figure it out using her natural mind. Fear often does this. When we experience something new from the Lord, we need to be mindful not to let fear shut down what Heaven is doing in our lives. Fear resists the move of God because it's outside of our comfort zone. It's calling us to new levels of faith and belief. It's opening our eyes to the reality of a very big already-in-motion story that God is at the center of and we get to participate in. Mary found herself caught right in the middle of this. Her response? She chooses to serve the word of the Lord. She would build her life around what God was saying to her instead of trying to bring His word down to her level.

DEFINING THE POWER

This may seem like a strange comparison, but track with me for just a moment. After Jesus rose from the dead and He was preparing to ascend back into Heaven, the disciples were trying to wrap their minds around the Great Commission He had just extended to them—to preach the Gospel and disciple nations through the teaching of Jesus.

Surely full of eager expectation about Jesus' victorious return, they asked Him the following question, "Lord, will You at this time restore the kingdom to Israel?" They still assumed that Jesus was going to immediately build a natural kingdom on earth and physically overthrow all of their oppressors. This idea made natural sense to the disciples, but it was not where Jesus was going. Amazing how we can miss a move of God sometimes because we are convinced He is going to move one way, when in fact He has the prerogative to move however He wants. It's not even that the disciples were entirely off!

Yes, a day would surely come when the Son of Man would split the sky and make everything wrong right in the earth, but that was not for right now. For now, Jesus was inviting His people to think differently and serve His commission as a spiritual community empowered by His Holy Spirit. How does Jesus respond?

He said to them, "It is not for you to know times or seasons that the Father has fixed by his own authority. But you will receive power when the Holy Spirit has come upon you, and you will be my witnesses in Jerusalem and in all Judea and Samaria, and to the end of the earth" (Acts 1:7-8).

In the same way Gabriel corrected Mary, Jesus corrected the disciples. Mary and the disciples surely wanted to understand how God was going to move in and through them. In both cases, though, Heaven gently corrects their perspectives and summons them to think higher.

For the disciples, Jesus was calling them into a reality that their minds could not fathom. They wanted a warrior, a conquering king to immediately overthrow and demolish Roman oppression. What Jesus was inviting them into was infinitely superior to this, as He promised they would receive Holy Spirit power, which makes it possible for ordinary men and women to do the same works that Jesus did (see John 14:12). Their target would not be the oppressive forces of a ruling government, but rather the powers of darkness in heavenly places (see Ephesians 6:12).

For Mary, Gabriel was calling her to partner with Heaven to host a move of God that would change history forever. All of the elements involved surely seemed preposterous. The Messiah being immaculately implanted into and hosted by the womb of a virgin teenager. I am just thankful she didn't allow her natural mind to dictate her response to God. Mary responded:

> "...As his servant, I accept whatever he has for me. May everything you have told me come to pass" (Luke 1:38 TPT).

What is Heaven calling you to say "Yes" to today? I have no doubt that on the other side of your obedience, like Mary and the disciples, will come the greatest God-adventure of your life! God wants to move on earth; He does this, primarily, through people who yield to Him and say, "Lord, move me, so You can move through me!"

PRAYER

Father, I give You my life afresh on Your terms, not mine. Whatever You want to do in me and through me, I say, "Yes!" Help me to think like Heaven. Renew my mind. May my thoughts agree with Your thoughts. Even though Your thoughts are not my thoughts, and Your ways are not my ways, Your Word also says that through the person of the Holy Spirit, I have access to the way You think! So whatever You are asking me to do today, I say, "Yes." I want to see You move. I want to see Your glory. I am not content living with a trickle or a portion of Your presence when You have promised rivers of living water.

MARY, DID YOU KNOW?

by Patricia King

…The Holy Spirit will come upon you, and the power of the Most High will overshadow you; therefore the child to be born will be called holy—the Son of God (Luke 1:35).

Mary was a young Jewish girl born into a poor family in Nazareth, which was an insignificant and demeaned town in that day.[1] It does not appear that she stood out in the midst of her peers and probably was rather unnoticed, but she had a pure, humble, and tender heart, and along with her family she was deeply devoted to God.

Eventually, Mary as a lovely young virgin was engaged to a man named Joseph, who like her, was not from a background of affluence but was a kind, stable, unpretentious and God-fearing man. Some historical accounts record that at the time of her engagement to Joseph, she was perhaps only fourteen years old. Mary was likely very excited about preparing her life for marriage with Joseph. She had her entire future ahead of her and like most young girls in their teens, she probably dreamed of being married, having children, and building a beautiful life as a family.

As she was in the season of preparation for marriage, the angel Gabriel shows up in her midst with a powerful prophetic word declaring an extremely vital destiny assignment that would influence all humankind for eternity.

Now in the sixth month the angel Gabriel was sent by God to a city of Galilee named Nazareth.… And having come in, the angel said to her, "Rejoice, highly favored one, the Lord is with you; blessed are you among women!" But when she saw him, she was troubled at his saying, and considered what manner of greeting this was. Then the angel said to her, "Do not be afraid, Mary, for you have found favor with God. And behold, you will conceive in your womb and bring forth a Son, and shall call His name Jesus. …Then Mary said to the angel, "How can this be, since I do not know a man?" And the angel answered and said to her, "The Holy Spirit will come upon you, and the power of the Highest will overshadow you; therefore, also, that Holy One who is to be born will be called the Son of God. …For with God nothing will be impossible" (Luke 1:26,28-31,34-35,37 NKJV).

This angelic visitation and prophetic word must have shaken Mary to the core and I wonder if she truly understood what it all meant. Most often when we receive a prophetic word, we have a witness to its Holy Spirit origin and we might even give our hearty, "Amen," but when the word unfolds in our lives and comes to pass, it is frequently quite different from what we thought or imagined.

In many ways, I'm sure Mary was shaken to her very core as she felt the awe of this visitation. She was being invited to give birth to and to raise the Son of God, but what would that entail? She had no experience in motherhood and would need to trust the Lord completely for His grace and wisdom. What a costly call as along with joy-filled experiences, there would be many painful moments she would face as she walked out the fulfillment of this powerful word and destiny assignment.

Mary submitted to a supernatural, God-inspired, Spirit-infused pregnancy that she knew would give rise to the ugliest of rumors and accusations, but that was only the beginning. She would be acquainted with grief as she watched her son face much opposition, slander, and pain. In spite of all of that was before her, Mary gave God her "YES": *"Let it be to me according to your word"* (Luke 1:38).

I'm confident that Jesus as a baby was like other infants in many ways. He needed to be fed, held, changed, bathed, and loved. I wonder when she looked at her little baby, if she truly grasped who He was and what He would accomplish. When Mary watched her young boy play with His peers, did she fully know the reality of who He was as the Savior of the world? When Jesus studied with the others, did she know that He was "The Truth"? When He healed the sick, cleansed the lepers, and raised the dead, did she fully know Him as the Anointed One? When she saw Him die on the Cross, did she know, did she understand the great power wrapped inside her loss?

Mary needed a revelation of Christ and His completed work on the Cross just like you and I do. She carried Him in her womb for nine months and brought Him forth into the world, but divine revelation and understanding unfolded over time as she walked with God one day at a time. She began to discover the fullness of what her womb brought forth. Probably many times she had to use the prophetic word to battle unbelief, fear, and times of being overwhelmed and feeling helpless. You and I are the same. When we are given a mandate from God, we have limited insight; but as we journey with Him, fuller understanding comes.

Mary was overshadowed by the Holy Spirit and she brought forth the life of God that impacted the universe for all eternity. That same potential is with you too. You might be thinking, *But I'm so insignificant… I'm not highly educated… I'm not very popular… I'm not well known…but I do love God.* This love makes you qualified. God is not looking for the most popular, the wisest, the most intellectual or gifted. He is looking for those who are willing to yield and give Him their YES.

With God all things are possible; and like Mary, He wants to overshadow you and bring forth His life into the world through you. You don't need Gabriel to show up—you have the living Word in print that you can receive into your soul. The Spirit was hovering over the darkness in the very beginning of time and then God declared the Word and light came.

God is hovering over you right now. Let His promises impregnate you with destiny fulfillment. You can't even begin to imagine the fullness of what God will birth through you. As the song, "Mary Did You Know," questions, you might also need to ponder the potential greatness of God's presence in you and through you.

Buddy Greene and Mark Lowry wrote the following song. It is one of my favorites and I want to share the anointed lyrics with you.

MARY DID YOU KNOW?

Mary did you know that your baby boy would one day walk on water?

Mary did you know that your baby boy would save our sons and daughters?

Did you know that your baby boy
has come to make you new?

This child that you've delivered, will soon deliver you?

Mary did you know that your baby boy
will give sight to a blind man?

Mary did you know that your baby boy
will calm a storm with his hand?

Did you know that your baby boy
has walked where angels trod?

When you kiss your little baby,
you kiss the face of God…Mary did you know?

The blind will see, the deaf will hear,
the dead will live again.

The lame will leap, the dumb will speak,
the praises of the Lamb.

Mary did you know that your baby boy
is Lord of all creation?

Mary did you know that your baby boy
would one day rule the nations?

Did you know that your baby boy
is heaven's perfect Lamb?

That sleeping child you're holding is
The Great "I Am"…Mary did you know?[2]

PRAYER

Heavenly Father, I believe all things are possible with You. I invite You to overshadow me with Your Spirit and create in me a sense of destiny and purpose that will bring glory to Your name for all eternity. I give You my "YES" to everything You desire to do through me. I humble myself…I yield…I love. Amen.

PATRICIA KING is a respected apostolic leader, evangelist, author, television host, media producer, and sought-after speaker who has given her life for the advancement of God's Kingdom. She is founder of Patricia King Ministries and Women in Ministries Network and cofounder of XPmedia.com. Patricia and her husband, Ron, have two adult sons and three grandchildren and live in Maricopa, Arizona.

ENDNOTES

1. "Mary the Mother of Jesus Biography," *Inspirational Christians,* posted by Steve Fortosis; https://www.inspirationalchristians .org/bible-characters/mary-the-mother-of-jesus-biography/; accessed May 16, 2019.

2. "Mary, Did You Know?" Written by Buddy Greene, Mark Lowry; Lyrics © Warner/Chappell Music, Inc., Capitol Christian Music Group.

THE GIFT OF PRESENCE

by Daniel Kolenda

When we celebrate Advent, we celebrate the truth of all truths. We call to mind the core teaching of the everlasting Gospel and the most transformative event in the history of the world. Simply put, we celebrate the Incarnation, when God's eternal Son became a human being and lived among us. Our finite minds can hardly grasp the grandeur of this statement—its mystery, its glory, its grace.

Could there be a more perfect Person than Jesus Christ? Can there be any other foundation to our salvation? "The Word who became flesh" reigns over every religion and philosophy as the perfection of truth. It is the heart and soul of our Gospel.

The Incarnation's magnificence should stun us into silent awe. It should also ignite us into burning adoration. Yet we can become so ensnared by the secularization of Christmas, or get so familiar with the biblical story that we lose sight of the wonder—the sheer impossibility that abides right at the center of our faith.

Pause and think about this for a moment. By the Holy Spirit, the pre-existent Son of God came into the womb of a young virgin. He experienced humanity on every possible level, from conception to death and everything in between. But He also remained the Person He had always been from eternity. His divine nature did not conflict with His human nature. Nor did the human clash with the divine. Somehow these two realities blended to perfection in a young Galilean known as "Yeshua."

It's as if God designed humans so He could one day become one of them. What can we say to these things? The Sovereign Creator became part of His creation. The Judge of the earth laughed with friends and played in the streets of Nazareth. The Giver of Life died on a cross and rose again from the grave...all as a human being.

But this is what I really want us to see. It's not just that Jesus was both divine and human. It's *why* He was both divine and human. The Incarnation occurred for a specific reason. God wanted to give us the ultimate gift. He wanted to give us Himself. He wanted to give us His presence. The very word "Advent" refers to Christ's coming or presence. When Isaiah prophesies that a virgin would be with child and bear a son, he also prophesies the son's name: Immanuel, which means God with us (Isaiah 7:14). When John proclaims that the Word became flesh, he also proclaims that He dwelt among us (John 1:14). Both writers give the full message. God's Son became human for the express purpose of being with us. That is the Gospel of Christmas. It's about the Presence.

God's human presence is the foundation of our faith. He could not save us unless He first came to us as a Man. But presence is not just the foundation of our faith. It is also the goal of our faith. We were saved by His presence, for the Presence. God saved us so He could give us Himself. The incarnate Son atoned for our sins and rose to new life so we could forever be present to one another in eternal fellowship.

There's nothing like "presence." It's a powerful, exquisite word. True presence is the opposite of absence. Presence evokes deep feelings of love, friendship, fellowship, and intimacy. It speaks of belonging and closeness. It touches the deepest places of our souls where we need family connection with God Himself. So, the Gospel embedded in Christmas declares that God recognized this need, and gave Himself to fill it.

Our hearts yearn for presence. Ironically, our digital world has done much both to connect us as well as isolate us. On the one hand, technology allows us to be more present to people even when we're far away. Social media and video calls actually enable us to connect even when we are separated by time zones. That's a wonderful gift.

On the other hand, technology can become a substitute for actual presence. God designed humans to live where our bodies actually are, not merely on cyberspace. We need physical proximity. An image can be a temporary provision, but it is not the reality itself. We must be physically near one another. We must be physically near God. He could not afford to send an angel or text message. He had to come in person. There is simply no substitute for presence.

Physical nearness creates an emotional warmth that we need. God designed us for presence with other humans. How much more has He designed us for presence with Him! Listen to John's testimony about the years he spent with Jesus: *"That which was from the beginning, which we have heard, which we have seen with our eyes, which we have looked upon, and our hands have handled, concerning the Word of life"* (1 John 1:1 NKJV). Notice how John took care to explain the full range of presence: hearing, seeing, looking intently, and touching. Jesus was totally present with His disciples. John's witness to Jesus flowed out of a mutual fellowship that could not be replaced by anything.

Consider Jesus' own teaching: *"**Where** two or three are **gathered** together in My name, **I am there** in the midst of them"* (Matthew 18:20 NKJV). It doesn't get any clearer than that. Jesus refers to a literal location, and a physical meeting and He refers to His own physical presence in that specific location. His presence in our gatherings depends partly on our presence to one another! Presence invites Presence. There's no substitute for the Presence.

The whole story of the Bible is about God's manifest Presence. In the beginning, Genesis tells us that the Lord was *"walking in the garden in the cool of the day"* (Genesis 3:8). He was physically present and longed for fellowship with His children (Genesis 3:9). Then at the end, Revelation tells us the goal of all history: *"Look! God's home is now among his people! He will live with them…"* (Revelation 21:3 NLT). At the beginning, end, and everywhere in between, we read about Presence.

God's whole plan for the world centers on His Presence. It's the message of the Bible, and the heart of the Gospel. That is why it's so important to push past the frenzy of commercialism and discern the purpose of Advent. Don't let the world dilute the purity of the season. Christmas embodies the Gospel message: God became human and made a way for us to come to Him. Now those who believe the Gospel have His Presence again in the Holy Spirit. The "Gospel of Christmas" declares the whole story of the Presence.

THE PRESENCE LOVES

God came into the world, alive and in person, because of His undying love for us. We sometimes forget this simple truth. But the Incarnation proves that God loves us deeply. When God loves, He makes a covenant. His love is not a temporary love that fizzles when times get tough or His needs are not met. No, God's love is eternal. It compels Him to bind Himself to His beloved forever. Part of such a covenant is His promise to give Himself to us as the Presence. *"I will dwell in them and walk among them. I will be their God, and they shall be My people"* (2 Corinthians 6:16 NASB).

Even throughout the Old Testament, God's love drove Him to come near His people. His fellowship with men like Abraham and Moses must have been too holy to behold. Yahweh appeared in human form to Abraham (Genesis 18:1-2), and was physically present to Moses in the cloud and on the mountain (Exodus 33:9-11,19-23; 34:1-9). What extraordinary moments! Yahweh longed to spend time with His children in person, just as He did in the garden.

Yet even these glorious moments were provisional manifestations. God promised that, one day, He would dwell permanently among His people. Before that, there were limits to the Presence. Moses begged to see God's glory, but he could not (Exodus 33:18-20). A veil separated the Holy of Holies from the Holy Place. And only the priests could go in to minister. There were restrictions to the Presence.

But when the fullness of time came, all barriers were torn down. God the Son came in the flesh and *"we saw His glory, glory as of the only begotten from the Father, full of grace and truth"* (John 1:14 NASB). The disciples saw what Moses begged to see. God finally fulfilled His covenant of love. He became present to His people as one of us.

THE PRESENCE SACRIFICES

But that was not enough. The Son did not become human to live here for thirty-three years and then leave. God's burning, covenantal love would not be satisfied with mere visitation. He longed for habitation. He wanted to create a scenario where we could be joined together forever. He had to do that, however, at His own expense. Jesus, the incarnate Son of God, came as a human so He could die and shed His precious blood. The sin that separated us and made us orphans could only be washed away by that divine-human blood (Acts 20:28). The Presence had to die.

We do not normally think of Presence in terms of suffering and sacrifice. For Jesus' Jewish disciples, presence meant something quite positive. It meant the Messiah would come, overthrow Israel's enemies, establish God's Kingdom on earth, and rededicate the temple. Then God would dwell among His people in unsurpassed glory. They did not expect the Presence to be beaten and murdered on a cross.

Likewise, we charismatics think of presence in terms of an atmosphere of sweetness, weeping, laughter, healing, or signs and wonders. We speak of the air suffused with God's palpable glory. We envision a meeting with exhilaration, worship, and joy. And we should.

But to fulfill the purpose of Advent, the Presence also had to walk through darkness. How could we be delivered from death, eternal separation, unless the Presence went there on our behalf? So yes, the Son of God's Presence meant fellowship with His people. But it also meant rejection and death. Otherwise He would only have been able to visit. Then He would be isolated from us forever, which is the very opposite of presence.

The body that housed the eternal Son of God died a brutal death on the Cross. But that Man has been raised from the dead and glorified. He now remains in a glorified human body forever. Yet even that glorified body—His eternal, human tent—bears scars. Those scars remind us of the Christmas Gospel. The Presence suffered death to deliver us from sin. Now we can have the Presence forever.

THE PRESENCE ABIDES

Advent celebrates the incarnate Presence who came to die. But it should also celebrate the Spirit's Presence who came to abide. The first Presence paved the way for the second Presence. The incarnate God came into the world. But the abiding God came into our hearts. To me, this truth should be as much a part of our Advent reflection as the Incarnation. I know there is a separate day on the Christmas calendar to celebrate Pentecost. But I'm not concerned so much with the calendar as I am with the Presence.

The Son of God became human so He could die and give us the Holy Spirit. It's not enough for us to talk about the facts of God's historical presence. We must also commit ourselves to be people of the abiding Presence! Talk is cheap. The Holy Spirit Presence in us desires to express Himself through us. To me, this is the ultimate meaning of Advent. Why should we recount the facts of Advent, but not demonstrate the abiding Presence of Advent?

To be Spirit-filled people is to be people marked by the Presence. Truly born again, Pentecostal and Charismatic people should celebrate the Advent season in all its fullness. The Christian Church is unique among all people and religions. It consists of humans, but not only humans. God Himself is present in the Church by the Spirit. The Church is the people of the Presence. *"Do you not know that you are the temple of God and that the Spirit of God dwells in you?"* (1 Corinthians 3:16 NKJV).

Listen to the Lord's conversation with Moses:

*"**My Presence will go with you**, and I will give you rest." Then he [Moses] said to Him, "If Your Presence does not go with us, do not bring us up from here. For how then will it be known that Your people and I have found grace in Your sight, except You go with us? So we shall be separate, Your people and I, from all the people*

who are upon the face of the earth" (Exodus 33:14-16 NKJV).

We should operate from the same conviction.

The Presence is the single element that distinguishes us from everyone else. That is why the Bible issues these commands to *"Walk by the Spirit… Be filled with the Spirit… Pray in the Spirit… Worship in the Spirit"* (Galatians 5:16; Ephesians 5:18; 6:18; John 4:24; Philippians 3:3). As the temple of the Holy Spirit, we should be intentional to obey these scriptural commands.

You and I are called to fellowship with the Holy Spirit. We have the power to pray in other tongues. Scripture instructs us to lay our hands on the sick in Jesus' name, and they will be healed. We can develop the Spirit's holy character and bear His Christlike fruit. When we gather together, God enables us to prophesy to one another. These are marks of the Presence that make us incandescent.

INVITATION

Advent is not just an event; it is our experience. Let's act like it. In the spirit of the Christmas season, let's be people of the Presence.

DANIEL KOLENDA is a missionary evangelist who has led more than 21 million people to Christ face to face through massive open-air evangelistic campaigns in some of the most dangerous, difficult, and remote locations on earth. As the successor to world-renowned Evangelist Reinhard Bonnke, Daniel is the president and CEO of Christ for All Nations, a ministry that has conducted some of the largest evangelistic events in history, has published over 190 million books in 104 languages, and has offices in ten nations around the world. He also hosts an internationally syndicated television program.

"FIND ME!"

by Ana Werner

ind Me," I heard Jesus' voice call out to me one day.

I'll never forget that morning. It was one of those days when everything that could go wrong, *went wrong*. My five-year-old daughter woke up in a bad mood that morning and was making life anything but fun. My two-year-old son was dive-bombing his body off the couch, pretending he was a torpedo. I had mistakenly forgotten that I had planned an event that day, and this was the day my husband left early for business. The list of stresses that morning went on and on, as I looked at a large pile of dishes that were also waiting for me.

Maybe you are not in a season in life with small children at home. Maybe you are not married either. Whatever season of life you are in, I do know that we all can relate to feeling overwhelmed at times. Life can get hectic in the season of Christmas, and when stresses increase so does our own fleshly, human nature. I know that I was anything but feeling peaceful that morning.

When I think of the birth of Jesus and the wonder behind it, I can't help but stop and think about Mary and Joseph's journey of faith. They found God in midst of the most chaotic of environments, and followed His direction. Can you imagine it? Just stop and imagine you are part of their story that happened over two thousand years ago.

It says in Matthew 1:20-21 (NASB) that an angel of the Lord appeared to Joseph in a dream saying, *"Joseph, son of David, do not be afraid to take Mary as your wife; for the Child who has been conceived in her is of the Holy Spirit. She will bear a Son; and you shall call His name Jesus, for He will save His people from their sin."*

We have to stop and wonder at the mystery of Jesus being placed in a young teenage virgin who is about to be married. Of all people, why did God choose Mary and Joseph as His Son's parents? Do you think they were totally prepared? NOPE! We know Joseph was a little frightened by the whole idea after Mary told him, and was planning on sending her away secretly and divorcing her. But God intervened, giving direction to an unprepared young man whose obedience changed history and the destiny of all humankind.

Then Caesar Augustus called for a census to be taken of all people in the Roman empire, so Joseph and Mary have to make a long journey during her last trimester of pregnancy back to Bethlehem. (I just can't even imagine sitting on a donkey in my last month of pregnancy!) Did it seem like the right timing for all of this? NOPE!

Yes, it fulfilled all the prophecies, but God could have chosen a different moment, a more peaceful one, in the span of time for this miracle birth to take place.

Then the Bible says in Luke 2:7 (NASB) that Mary *"gave birth to her firstborn son; and she wrapped Him in cloths, and laid Him in a manger, because there was no room for them in the inn."* It is so humbling to think that Jesus left His throne in Heaven and came to earth and was born in the most stinky and unlikely of places, for *us*. Does it seem like the right place for all of this to be happening? NOPE!

And yet He came, bringing peace on earth and good will toward all people.

As, I stood over the sink that day, frantically scrubbing those dishes, my mind raced trying to come up with a game plan for the day, for all the tasks that lay ahead of me.

And just then, Jesus interrupted my thoughts, "Find Me."

I was instantly taken into a vision. I found myself in a beautiful garden, and there was Jesus walking right toward me.

I instantly began to weep. I didn't need to say it; He knew the stress and pressure I felt I was under. Being that close to my King Jesus just melted my heart.

Stopping, He looked at me. Those tender, loving eyes looked into mine. They seemed to say, "I know. I know."

Then He spoke.

"It's only as overwhelming as you make it," He said to me. "Lean into Me, beloved."

Instantly, I felt the pressure of the chaos and stress lift. I felt peace come over me and wrap around me like a blanket. I ended up repenting for agreeing with stress and feeling overwhelmed. I found myself then declaring over that sink of messy dishes Philippians 4:13 (NKJV), *"I can do all things through Christ who strengthens me."*

The Lord has brought me back to that encounter several times throughout my lifetime, at times that I need it the most.

As the busyness of this season creeps upon us, let's stop and take a moment to meditate on the miracle of Christmas. Mary and Joseph may have not been the most prepared for the task at hand, it may have seemed like the most unlikely of places and worst timing ever, but yet God chose them and that timing to interrupt our world and bring *peace.*

INVITATION

*So whatever task you find yourself in today, choose peace. Not by your strength alone will you get through today, but as you lean in to the Father and give Him your burdens, He will give you strength. Your ability to hear God, even in the midst of this moment, will be what carries you through. "Why me, God?" you might ask. It is less about the **why**, and more about the **how** right now that's important. Your willingness to trust Him when you can't even see how you will get through it all. The timing may seem off or wrong, but can you believe that God is about to do something incredible in your life? You were created to shine and carry peace in the midst of chaos and darkness. Just as Mary and Joseph did, this is your moment to shine! Shine, beloved!*

ANA WERNER and her husband, Sam reside in Missouri with their two beautiful children, and are the associate directors of the Heartland Healing Rooms in Lees Summit. Ana travels internationally and equips people to see in the Spirit, move in the prophetic, and experience healing and deliverance through her ministry. Her transparency as she shares the realities and experiences she has had in Heaven, brings the Holy Spirit, the love of the Father, and the power of God into the room when she speaks. Ana is passionate about leading people into encountering Jesus' heart.

For more information visit: anawerner.org.

MY GRANDMOTHER'S BIBLE

by Karen Wheaton

s a child, during the sometimes long sermons at church, I loved to entertain myself by looking at the pictures scattered throughout my grandmother's thick Bible. With vivid color and graphic detail, each picture came alive to me and left me in awe and wonder at its meaning and message. These all became portraits hung in the gallery of my memory that I frequently find myself strolling through with the same intrigue and question I had as a child. It is as though each painting is still speaking, weaving into one storyline a message from the Artist Himself.

In the beginning of the gallery is the beautiful portrait of Eden, the garden of God. The bright green grass, the cloudless blue sky, and the flowers of every color imaginable reflect the magnificent creativity of their Creator. Animals of every kind walk about with no animosity or fear, for the atmosphere itself appears to be perfect love.

Back in the distance is the man, Adam, and his counterpart, Eve, conveniently standing behind a hedge of shrubbery. They are the caretakers of this lush garden, but far more than that, they are actually the son and daughter of the Creator Himself. Unlike the rest of creation, they look like Him. They reflect His glory, bearing the very image of their Father. He gives them authority and dominion over all His creation. As He and they co-labor together, He delights in hearing the name and identity Adam gives each animal He had so artistically crafted.

With limitless imagination and possibility, they dream together—God and Adam and Eve—in this beautiful place, sharing deep intimacy as they walk and talk in the cool of the day. This unspoiled scene in my memory's gallery tells me the way our Father wants His world to be—a place of perfect beauty, perfect communion, and perfect love.

The next picture reveals the flawless features of Eve as she looks with contemplative intrigue at the enticing fruit she is holding between her slender fingers. Very near to her is the figure of a cunning serpent entwined around the tree of which she has wandered too closely. Adam and Eve have been given boundless access to this paradise with the exception of this one tree—the tree of knowing good and evil. According to the words of their Father, to eat the fruit of this tree will result in certain death. With no paradigm for death, it seems harmless enough to her to draw near and gaze upon its compelling beauty. It is then she notices the serpent that seems to live in its branches.

Since Adam and Eve have been made caretakers of their Father's creation, to communicate with an animal or serpent is nothing unusual, really. All seems quite normal until the serpent begins to speak of things that question the validity of her Father's word, thus undermining His authority and questioning the very depth of His character.

"Did God say?" is the serpent's query. This beguiles her to doubt the intent of her Father's command. She is now convinced the serpent is right. God cannot be fully trusted. She tastes the fruit and invites Adam to share in its deceitful delight. In that moment, their eyes are opened to a world of darkness, shame, and sin. Their glorious bodies are now infected by the pull of death that is calling them back to the dust from whence they came. Their love for their Father has now turned to fear of their Father. For the first time, they run and hide when they hear Him calling, "Adam! Adam! Where are you?"

I can still remember the sadness I felt as a child when I looked at the next picture. Adam and Eve are being made to leave the beautiful garden. Wearing garments made from the skins of animals, they are bent low, hands covering their faces, weeping, as they leave the presence of their Father to follow the new master they have chosen through their disobedience. The land before them looks dark and uncertain. Adam works by the sweat of his brow to break up the dirt that has now been cursed with thorns and thistles. Eve experiences the pain of bringing life into a world that has been cursed by the choice she made.

They miss the ease and glory of the garden, but most of all, they miss their Father. The sound of His voice, the joy in His laughter, their walks together in the cool of the day are all becoming a distant memory. They try to create words that will describe to their children and their children's children the face of their Father and the world they once knew. Adam and Eve want their children to know Him, too. But how will they know Him? They have been born spiritually blind to His world and spiritually deaf to His voice.

It is here we would think the gallery would end. Surely, the final picture would be this one—Adam and Eve walking away forever from their Father and His world, living only to survive until they and all their sons and daughters are consumed by the curse of death. After all, wouldn't it have been easier for the Father to have left them with the consequence of their disobedience? Couldn't He have simply gone back into His home in the heavens and forgotten they ever existed and created another world without them? Maybe so, but the story doesn't end that way. With each step down the gallery's corridor, the pictures continue to tell the story of a Father who never stops calling out to His sons and daughters, "I'm coming to save you!"

Turning the corner, we discover the story continues. Here, we have the portrait of the man who found grace in the Father's eyes. It is Noah, standing on the deck of his big boat with his arms lifted high in worship and covered by the rainbow of His Father's promise, "I'm coming to save you!"

Next, we pass the picture of a very old man standing behind an altar made of stone. In his right hand, he holds a dagger that has just been thrust into the air. Atop the altar, laid across the purposely placed wood, is a young man, his hands and feet tied as though he was a willing sacrifice. Looking carefully, we can see the anguished relief on the face of the aged father as he appears to hear a voice shouting from Heaven, "Abraham! Don't lay a hand on the boy! Now that I know you love Me, I will bless you!" The message behind the Father's request for Abraham's sacrifice is a loud and clear promise to all the sons and daughters of Adam, "I'm coming to save you!"

Coming to the next portrait, we see the masterpiece of the man, Moses. He is on his knees, holding stone tablets in his hands that appear to have been given to him straight from the hand of the Father Himself! Written on the tablets are laws that will teach and protect Moses and the children of Israel until they can come again into the Father's Kingdom. God requests that Moses build a tabernacle, a Most Holy Place, where He can dwell on the earth to be near the ones He loves once more. Separated only by the curtain that hangs in the Holy Place, the Father is among them. Once a year, as the High Priest enters behind the veil and atonement is made for the sins of the people, God proclaims His promise, "I'm coming to save you!"

Continuing in the gallery's narrative, we encounter the young David with his sling. It is whirling through the air, hurling the stone into the falling giant's head. Now we see Daniel, standing tall and straight, with his face heavenward, as the lions around him appear to be ready for a good night's sleep. But I must not forget one of my favorite scenes. Standing unafraid are three young men inside the fiery furnace, yet standing among them is a fourth Man, glowing with the glory of God!

Throughout the Old Testament, each picture resonates with the love of the Father intervening in the time of His children's trouble, defeating enemies that were too strong for them, and prophesying through each of them, "I'm coming to save you!"

Over four thousand years have passed since Adam and Eve walked away from Eden. The longing, searching heart of the Father has followed their offspring through the wilderness to the Promised Land. He has watched them worship other gods, pretending they never knew Him. He has endured their rebellion and longed for their repentance. He spoke through Isaiah, Jeremiah,

Micah, and Malachi—calling His children back to Himself for communion and fellowship—promising He would someday send a Deliverer, a Savior, a Messiah. Again and again, His voice rang out, "I'm coming to save you! I'm coming to save you!"

With a final turn in the gallery, we pass through empty corridors representing four hundred years of silence. Between the Old Testament and the New Testament, there is not one picture on the wall. Then, suddenly, as if out of nowhere, we see it! It's the picture all creation has longed to see, portrayed in a scene no one had ever imagined. A manger, complete with hay, animal stalls, and a dirt floor. Laying in the foreground are cows and sheep wondering about the unusual company with whom they are sharing their barn. To the right of the picture are perplexed shepherds, kneeling in worship. Standing to the side is Joseph and sitting on a bale of hay in front of him is Mary. But it is the One in the middle of the manger who has captured their gaze.

There, lying in an animal trough and wrapped in swaddling clothes, is the Baby. Contained within the small moving frame is the very essence of God. The sound of His first cry moves the heavens and earth, for it was this Voice that released their birth. Angels have filled the sky above the small barn. They all peer into the wonder of the moment and share the same thought, *What manner of love is this?*

Although prophets and angels could not comprehend its meaning, as a child, sitting there next to my grandmother, with her Bible stretched across my knees, I understood! Yes, I knew exactly what it meant—He came! He came! Just like He promised. He came to live among us, to understand the feeling of our infirmities, to bear our grief and carry our sin to His Cross. Yes, I understood. The Baby in this picture was born to die so we could live. He came to save us so we could return with Him, back to His beautiful world, and know again the eternal, unfailing love of our Father.

As the sermon neared its end, I would close my grandmother's Bible and listen as she lifted her sweet voice to join with the others gathered around her singing the song of invitation. As their voices became one, I'd close my eyes and hear the Voice within their voices still calling to the sons and daughters of Adam, "Come home, come home, ye who are weary come home. Softly and tenderly, Jesus is calling. Calling, oh sinner, come home."

He came so we could come home. With the faith of a child, I accepted the invitation.

REFLECTION

Say to those with fearful hearts, "Be strong, and do not fear, for your God is coming....

He is coming to save you" (Isaiah 35:4 NLT).

KAREN WHEATON is a seasoned Christian minister whose music and preaching has provoked listeners to pursue God in passionate worship for many years. Her first exposure came on the PTL Club in 1978. As a young lady of only 18, she traveled with the Spurrlows in the Festival of Praise, and by 1980 she launched her solo ministry, traveling with her own band and back-up singers, singing and preaching the gospel across the nation. Throughout the '80's Karen had the privilege of serving alongside some of the great ministers of that day.

Throughout the '90's Karen continued to work with other ministers, while increasingly traveling on her own as doors opened to sing and speak at various churches, prisons and women's conferences. In 1998 the emphasis of her ministry took a surprising turn as God called her to move back to her hometown of Hamilton, Alabama and to begin working with the youth of the community.

Today, she continues to travel and minister, but her efforts are primarily focused at the Ramp where thousands gather every year to be transformed by the presence of God and equipped to win their cities. Karen has given her life for the vision and mission of awakening. Part of this includes raising up spiritual sons and daughters, weekly teaching students at RSM and continually developing young men and women into the mature believers God has called them to be.

Behind the scenes, Karen's husband, Rick, functions as the CEO. Through his unwavering dedication and extensive administrative experience, Rick oversees the everyday operations of the Ramp. Previously working as Senior Vice President for Covenant Transport, Rick uses his business skills to direct ministry finances, RSM expansion, and future Ramp development. His focus to create an infrastructure, which is pleasing to God, continuously propels the ministry closer to the fulfillment of the vision. Rick's commitment to see this dream become a reality inspires the Ramp staff and constantly challenges them to reach for greater achievement.

Rick and Karen are laying down their lives to see a generation awakened. Believing for revival in the nations of the earth, they are passionately pursuing the dreams of God. They are visionaries of the Ramp's ever-expanding ministry, dreaming and giving their lives that the earth would be touched with a third great awakening.

CHRISTMAS IS NOT MAGICAL—IT'S SUPERNATURAL!

by Larry Sparks

This Christmas, the Lord is extending a *dare* to His people: "I dare you…." Dares from Heaven to earth are not flippant. They're not like adolescent dares from our childhood peers, where the reward for our risk was a mere high five. When Heaven extends a dare, the Lord seeks to partner with a willing, obedient vessel in order to release something into the earth. This year, the dare has everything to do with *how* we engage the spiritual airways during the Christmas season.

Is Christmas Magical?

No, there is no "magic of Christmas." I'm sure Disney and the Hallmark channel would disagree on this one. The reality is, *yes* there is something unique and special in the air when the calendar shifts the nations into this time of year. Why? No magic; just Scripture coming to pass. Psalm 22:3 reminds us that God inhabits the praises of His people. Imagine what this looks like on a global scale!

While there are many factors that contribute to the so-called "magic" of Christmas, perhaps the top contributor to there being a "different" atmosphere during this time of year is the blatant declaration of truth concerning the Messiahship of Jesus Christ. This comes through the Christmas carols that are being released into the airways in coffee shops, malls, gyms, etc.

Consider these familiar lyrics:

∗ "Glory to the newborn King!"

∗ "King forever, ceasing never"

∗ "Let earth receive her King!"

∗ "Remember Christ our Savior was born on Christmas Day to save us all from Satan's power"

In the same way we encourage people not to "go through the motions" as they sing popular praise choruses, we must provide this same encouragement during the Christmas season.

I believe the Lord has two assignments for us this Christmas: 1) Plug the power back in when it comes to our Christmas church gatherings and services; and 2) receive our assignments to partner with the intercessory declarations that are released over the airways through Christmas carols.

The Longing of Humanity— at Christmas and Always

Christmas carols contain some of the most powerful intercessory decrees and revelation about Jesus. Why, then, does it feel like when Christian culture transitions over to the Christmas calendar, we often go into "showtime" mode? In our quest to genuinely help connect people with God, we sadly abandon the very One—the Holy Spirit—who is the *only One* who can legitimately bridge the gulf between lost humankind and the holy God.

In our attempts to provide "non-offensive" experiences for people to be exposed to Jesus, we often disconnect from the supernatural power of the Spirit. He is the *only Source* who will ultimately satisfy the deep longing of *every* thirsty human heart. David recognized this in Psalm 63:1—we live in a *"a dry and weary land where there is no water."* Apart from an encounter with the living God, that's very true—there is no source of fulfillment for the cry of the human heart. And yet, even though nothing in the world can satisfy this longing, *"there is a River."*

Jesus announced in John 7 that there is a River residing within us. He's a Person called Holy Spirit, and He is meant to be released: *"Out of his heart will flow rivers of living water"* (John 7:38). The key word is *"Out."* Out of you, out of me, out of this community called the Church will flow the very life-giving, thirst-quenching water that has the potential to satisfy every desperate cry of a *"dry and thirsty land."*

If there was any time during the calendar year when the Holy Spirit should be moving with unusual power in our gatherings, it should be at Christmas. And yet, this is the very time when we tend to "mute" the supernatural in favor of something that will not offend "new people" or "people seeking a relationship with God." Have we forgotten that it's the Holy Spirit who bridges the gulf between lost humanity and God Almighty?

There is nothing wrong with our concerts and cantatas, productions and pageants. Enjoy the candle-lighting services and tree-lighting events! Preach the "Christmas themed" sermon series throughout the month of December! Integrate Christmas carols into the standard praise and worship sets.

But here is where Heaven's dare comes in. It's like when we start singing the "Christmas carols," we go into a different mode. Performance mode, maybe? Somehow, we see the Christmas carols as traditional fare of the season. We sing them with smiles on our faces and warmth in our hearts, sure, but little expectation of divine encounter. After all, "They're just Christmas carols." This is where we need to recapture the awe and wonder of the profound realities these carols announce!

WHAT SHUTS DOWN THE FLOW?

What shuts down the flow of supernatural power at Christmas? Immediately, the Lord reminded me of a Gospel account that is comparable to what we face during the Christmas season today.

In Mark chapter 6, Jesus comes into His hometown of Nazareth. On the Sabbath, He proceeds to teach in the synagogue. What an amazing scene: Nazareth was experiencing a divine visitation by the very Son of God! Consider the supernatural possibilities that were available to Nazareth because of the presence of Jesus. And yet, Nazareth missed its moment of divine visitation:

> ...*many who heard him were astonished, saying, "Where did this man get these things? What is the wisdom given to him? How are such mighty works done by his hands?"* (Mark 6:2)

We are meant to live astonished by the wonder of Jesus. Motivated by this level of awe, we would approach singing Christmas carols in a very different way. Rather than seasonal traditions, they would become impassioned anthems of praise. Awe and wonder incite genuine praise and worship, and thus create an atmosphere for God's power to move without restraint. On the other hand, familiarity pulls the plug on divine power. If only Nazareth *stayed* astonished by Jesus. If only we could *stay* astonished. What pulled the plug on divine power? In Nazareth back then, and for us today, the culprit is familiarity.

> *"Is not this the carpenter, the son of Mary and brother of James and Joses and Judas and Simon? And are not his sisters here with us?" And they took offense at him. And Jesus said to them, "A prophet is not without honor, except in his hometown and among his relatives and in his own household." And he could do no mighty work there, except that he laid his hands on a few sick people and healed them. And he marveled because of their unbelief...* (Mark 6:3-6).

He wasn't the Son of God, the Miracle Worker, or even the Prophet of the Lord. To these hometown folk, He was the carpenter, the son of Mary. Unbelief didn't make Jesus less powerful, it simply prevented the community in Nazareth from having an appropriate level of expectation of what Jesus could do in their midst. Nazareth could have experienced a divine visitation. The dead could have been raised, the sick healed, and the demonized delivered. The Kingdom could have come with dynamic power to that community. It did...and didn't. Jesus, the King of the Kingdom, had come.

UNBELIEF DOESN'T CHANGE JESUS' NATURE

Unbelief doesn't change Jesus' nature; it simply prevents those who embrace familiarity from experiencing His power. Likewise, our religious, traditional, familiar approach to the Christmas season has the potential to pull out the plug of divine power. The Holy Spirit is powerful—period. Our unbelief or familiarity with Him does not change Him; it simply changes what we have the potential to experience from Him.

The airwaves are ripe with possibility. As it was in Nazareth, so it is today. Will we be apathetic or awakened? Familiar or fascinated?

What would happen if we sang a familiar carol like "O Holy Night" from hearts of awe and expectation… and the lyrics became manifestation? Could you even imagine a church service at Christmastime where the entire congregation is gripped by the fear of the Lord and falls prostrate before the presence of God during the singing of carols?

✳ What if the church fell to its knees as the people sang these lyrics in worshipful adoration?

✳ What if the gathering became a "thin place," where Heaven and earth interacted with increased ease and intensity?

✳ What if we could literally hear "angel voices" and witness angelic activity in the midst of worshipping with these carols?

✳ What if we declared the lyrics "chains shall He break" and "in His name all oppression shall cease," and people experienced divine healing and supernatural deliverance?

I believe God is daring His people to welcome His Spirit, engage the Christmas season with Kingdom expectation, and partner with the declarations being released over the airways.

YOUR CALL TO BOOTS-ON-THE-GROUND INTERCESSION

You have influence into the environments you carry the Holy Spirit. Perhaps the greatest assignment the Lord extends to His people during this season, other than evangelism, is intercession. And it's boots-on-the-ground intercession. We're not in some prayer chamber, isolated from the world. God wants His Church right in the middle of where hurting people are. And where there are people, there are problems. There is torment. There is oppression. There is sickness. There is bitterness. There is family strife. There are broken marriages. There is seasonal depression. This is what people carry around with them into the environments you interact with *every day*.

INVITATION

What if the Christmas carols playing in the background became an opportunity for you to pray in agreement with the lyrics being sung? Ask the Holy Spirit to help you become a spiritual governor of the different atmospheres you come into contact with by: 1) hearing the lyrics being sung; 2) bringing your prayers into agreement with the lyrics; and 3) asking the Holy Spirit to show you how to partner with the truth being released through these carols to see His Kingdom come this Christmas.

THE PLAN OF ALL PLANS REVEALED THROUGH THE CHRISTMAS STORY

by Kyle Winkler

We all have our Christmas traditions. A favorite of mine is to search for a song that might move me in a special way for the season. Usually it's a particular line or two that first catches my attention. One year, the simple verse, "God and sinners reconciled" from "Hark! The Herald Angels Sing" brought me to my knees in worship. Another year, the proclamation "in His Name, all oppression shall cease" from "O Holy Night" stirred my soul.

But most recently, the start of "God Rest Ye Merry Gentlemen" provoked my praise. Do you know it? It goes, "Remember, Christ our Savior was born on Christmas day to save us all from Satan's power when we were gone astray." Think about those words. Have you ever considered the purpose of Christmas having anything to do with victory over the enemy? Most haven't. Yet this is precisely what the apostle John declared was the purpose of Jesus' arrival on earth: *"...the Son of God came to destroy the works of the devil"* (1 John 3:8 NLT).

As I reflected upon the lyrics that December, the Holy Spirit led me on a journey through the Christmas story to understand how every detail is prophetic of that purpose. Follow me now through Luke's account of Jesus' birth to be awed by how it all reveals the plan of all plans.

THE FALLEN WORLD OF THE FIRST CHRISTMAS

Let's begin on the same page about the world into which Jesus was born. It was a world under the influence of the devil. In short, when satan deceived the first couple to sin, they effectively handed him the dominion that was originally intended for humankind (Genesis 1:26,28). From that very moment, creation was fallen. For the first time, death entered, and with it, all of its counterparts: sickness, suffering, disaster, and more. Awful as these are, they are only the consequences of satan's greatest work, which was separating God's children from an intimate relationship with Him.

The only solution to restore something from death is to cover it with perfect life. The Bible reveals, *"the life of the body is in its blood"* (Leviticus 17:11 NLT). As a fix, so to speak, God eventually instituted the law of atonement through which the sins of His people would be covered by the blood of a pure, spotless lamb.

To be sure, animal sacrifice was never God's perfect will. But He used it as a temporary solution to point to what was to come—the redemption plan He devised before creation's conception. This was the plan of which the prophets foretold, and the apostle Peter confirmed: *"It was the precious blood of Christ, the sinless, spotless Lamb of God. God chose him as your ransom long before the world began..."* (1 Peter 1:19-20). As we're about to explore, the first Christmas marks the moment this Word became flesh.

THE PROPHETIC PURPOSE OF BETHLEHEM

At that time the Roman emperor, Augustus, decreed that a census should be taken throughout the Roman Empire. ...All returned to their own ancestral towns to register for this census. And because Joseph was a descendant of King David, he had to go to Bethlehem in

Judea, David's ancient home. He traveled there from the village of Nazareth in Galilee. He took with him Mary, to whom he was engaged, who was now expecting a child (Luke 2:1-5 NLT).

Previously known as the city in which David was born and later crowned king of Israel, Jesus' birthplace of Bethlehem is only six miles south of Jerusalem, where He would later be crucified. Because of a prophecy foretold by Micah, for some seven hundred years, God's people looked to this little town of Bethlehem as the birthplace of their long-awaited Messiah (see Micah 5:2).

One of my favorite promises of God is that He orders the steps of His people (Psalm 37:23). How Mary and Joseph found themselves delivering our Messiah in the place that was foretold provides perhaps the perfect example of God's faithfulness to this promise.

Because Joseph was a descendant of the royal line of King David, the census ordered by the emperor required he make the several-day journey from his current residence in Nazareth to Bethlehem, the home of his lineage. But the story notes that Mary makes the journey, too. Surely not because such a trip would be enjoyable in the final days of her pregnancy, but likely out of obligation to enroll as the new wife of Joseph.

Pause to marvel at the precise timing of these events. Much longer in Nazareth and Jesus would've been born somewhere else. Yet by no planning on Mary's part, nor any intent by the emperor to fulfill prophecy, Mary and

Joseph are brought to Bethlehem. And while there, she goes into labor.

Isn't this how many of us find God's plans fulfilled in our lives, too? More often than not, it's the inconvenient events, frustrating circumstances, or the people who wander across our paths at the strangest moments that end up working like a Divine hand to lead us right where we need to be.

Undoubtedly, Bethlehem was right where Mary and Joseph needed to be, right at the right moment. But it was more than only because Joseph's lineage happened to originate there. No, Bethlehem was strategically chosen to be part of the plan from the beginning. As only God could know, events were orchestrated throughout the centuries, so that by the time of Jesus' birth, it was the city where lambs purchased for sacrifice in the temple were born and raised. In fact, every firstborn male lamb in Bethlehem was set aside to later be delivered to Jerusalem.[1] And certainly, without coincidence, so was the Lamb of God.

A SETTING SUITABLE FOR A LAMB

And while they were there, the time came for her baby to be born. She gave birth to her firstborn son. She wrapped him snugly in strips of cloth and laid him in a manger, because there was no lodging available for them (Luke 2:6-7 NLT).

As you just read, while in Bethlehem, Mary went into labor. But with the crowds flocking to the region for the census, the inns were filled, leaving Mary and Joseph in the dilemma of where to deliver Jesus. Of course, labor doesn't allow much opportunity to search for alternative options. With time running out, the expectant couple had to settle without optimal accommodations—in a shelter for the animals of guests staying at the inn.[2]

Imagine the scene. Jesus didn't enter this earth with the fanfare and fixings fit for a king. No, He came into a world busy of hustle and bustle, which essentially instructed, "Move along. Don't show up here. We have no room for you."

Possibly more inconvenient than a pregnant woman traveling eighty bumpy miles for a census, was delivering a baby among dirty, stinky animals. Those raised in small towns and farming communities surely know the unpleasant realities of such an environment. Nobody would pick an animal shelter as the delivery room for any infant, much less the most important one. But God did.

As the story goes, after Jesus' birth, He was placed in a manger. Not the wooden kind often depicted in our modern Nativity scenes, but a *phante* (Greek), which is a feeding trough for animals. It's unthinkable. The Son of the Most High, who was destined to sit on the throne of His ancestor David, was born in the humblest of places—a shelter made for animals, placed inside a feeding trough, and wrapped with mere strips of cloth.

As rough as this environment was for a birth, yet again God used an inconvenience as a prophetic setting for Jesus' destiny. A manger—a feeding trough—is the suitable place for a lamb. Fittingly then, it's where the Lamb of God spent His first days.

SHEPHERDS AWAIT
THEIR NEW ARRIVAL

That night there were shepherds staying in the fields nearby, guarding their flocks of sheep. Suddenly, an angel of the Lord appeared among them, and the radiance of the Lord's glory surrounded them. They were terrified, but the angel reassured them. "Don't be afraid!" he said. "I bring you good news that will bring great joy to all people. The Savior—yes, the Messiah, the Lord—has been born today in Bethlehem, the city of David! And you will recognize him by this sign: You will find a baby wrapped snugly in strips of cloth, lying in a manger" (Luke 2:8-12).

A region known for raising lambs should also be known for shepherds. Bethlehem was no exception. Every year, when autumn turned to winter, the natural time for sheep to give birth, known as lambing season, began. Of course, the job of a shepherd is to watch for predators that might ravage their flocks. But during this time, they also tended to the birth of infant lambs to ensure they were born without defects and were pro-tected from injury.[3]

While on their night watch, perhaps awaiting the arrival of a newborn lamb, God broke in, and the radiance of His glory pierced through the darkness with a dazzling light. The shepherds were understandably startled, but God's peace was delivered through a heavenly messenger proclaiming *"good news that will bring great joy to all people."*

Perhaps the full significance of this news wasn't caught at the time. But it was as if God said to these Jewish shepherds, "Out of your long night, your long-awaited, final, sacrificial Lamb is born. Now go quickly to do what you were destined for—inspect My Lamb and you will see that He is perfect—pure, spotless, and without defect."

> *Suddenly, the angel was joined by a vast host of others—the armies of heaven—praising God and saying, "Glory to God in highest heaven, and peace on earth to those with whom God is pleased." When the angels had returned to heaven, the shepherds said to each other, "Let's go to Bethlehem! Let's see this thing that has happened, which the Lord has told us about." They hurried to the village and found Mary and Joseph. And there was the baby, lying in the manger* (Luke 2:13-16).

THE PLAN OF ALL PLANS

Reflect upon what we've just explored. Could the details of the Christmas story be the product of mere coincidence? Hardly. The account is packed with prophetic pictures all pointing to the plan of all plans that God established long before creation began.

It's a praise-provoking picture! Some two thousand years ago, just before the first Christmas, God looked down upon His once-perfect, now-fallen creation to see a people in darkness, drudging through brokenness. He saw the pains of sickness and disability, the wounds of failed relationships and separated families, the shame of promiscuity and regrettable acts. He grieved over the sad state He never wanted, but one that was the result of the works of the devil.

Then God did something about it. He implemented His plan. God sent His one and only Son Jesus to enter our wounded world as a human with all its limits, in the lowliest of places, to be executed for the redemption and restoration of a people who had no room for Him.

It may seem unfathomable, but it's true. The Christmas story foretells the plan of He who became our final, sacrificial Lamb, all in order to destroy the devil's works and the ultimate consequence of them—separation from God.

REFLECTION

From cradle to Cross, Jesus accomplished His mission to restore our intimate relationship with the Father. Because of Christmas, as it was in the beginning, the

Father is now and forevermore, Emmanuel—God with you, God with me, God with us!

KYLE WINKLER is the founder of Kyle Winkler Ministries, author of *Silence Satan* and *Activating the Power of God's Word,* and creator of the highly acclaimed mobile app, Shut Up, Devil! Through his speaking engagements and broadcasts, Kyle is known for using his own story to boast in the power of God's Word for victory over fear, insecurity and issues of the past. Kyle holds a Master of Divinity in Biblical Studies from Regent University.

Endnotes

1. Brodie and Brock Thoene, *Why a Manger* (Middlebury, VT: Parable Publishing, 2006).

2. Kenneth Bailey, "The Manger and the Inn," Associates for Biblical Research, http://www.biblearchaeology.org/research/new-testament-era/2803-the-manger-and-the-inn.

3. "The Season of Jesus' Birth—When?" Discover the Bible Lands, http://www.discoverthebiblelands.com/the-season-of-jesus-birth-when-was-it/; accessed May 17, 2019.

GOD KNOWS HOW

by Tim Sheets

[Says the angel, Gabriel,] *"Not one promise from God is empty of power, for nothing is impossible with God!" Then Mary responded, saying, "This is amazing! I will be a mother for the Lord! As his servant, I accept whatever he has for me. May everything you have told me come to pass." And the angel left her* (Luke 1:37-38 TPT).

The wonder, majesty, and spectacular details of the Christmas story have amazed humanity for centuries. The most magnificent beings in the entire universe are involved—Father God, Holy Spirit, and Jesus. Heaven's mightiest angels also play an integral part. Gabriel, an archangel who stands in God's presence in the very throne room of Heaven, actually comes to earth and appears to Mary and Joseph, imparting messages that instruct the narrative. Michael, the most powerful angel ever created, also participates in the story. As an angel prince over Heaven's angel armies, Michael and his forces patrol the regions of Judea in watchful protection of Christ's birth.

Lucifer and his fallen angels were not to interfere in any way, shape, or form, and they did not; Michael, Gabriel, and the angelic armies saw to that. The plans, which had been hidden from the foundation of the earth, were unfolding in brilliant pageantry.

Mary had no idea what was going to happen. She was not expecting a message to be personally spoken to her by the number-one angel messenger in all of Heaven's hosts. She was caught off guard, as most of us would certainly be. Gabriel introduced himself to Mary, speaking words that would surprise anyone, *"You have been chosen to give birth to the Son of God."* This statement reveals an amazing truth—God has a plan for each of us individually, that we know nothing about, but in which the Holy Spirit and His angels are engaged.

We don't know how long Mary had to ponder this message. We simply know that she was perplexed and confused about what this could mean, and ultimately asked the question that so many of us deal with at times. How can this be? Gabriel answers her question by stating, *"With God, nothing is impossible."*

The word "nothing" in Gabriel's statement does not mean *zero.* It is the Greek word *rhema,* which speaks of a word of promise that the Holy Spirit causes to come alive to you. It is a word God gives us through our pursuit of a personal relationship with Him. This is why it is so important to meditate on God's Word, thinking on its meaning and allowing Him time to bring revelation of that word to you personally. Gabriel literally said, "Nothing God promises you is impossible."

This principle is vital. Spend time in God's presence, praying, declaring, and laying claim to what He says, until you know it has been "life-d" into you.

Implementing this truth allows us to cultivate an atmosphere where we can hear God speak to us. No word that God gives you through relationship with Him is impossible.

The word "impossible," in the original language, is the Greek word *adunateo*, meaning impotence, weakness, or inability to produce. Mary asked the question, "How can I become pregnant?" Gabriel answered, "Nothing God promises you is impotent." Nothing He promises is too weak to be accomplished. In other words, every word He says to you is potent with power to produce.

Gabriel lived in the spirit realm; Mary, like us, lived in the natural realm. These two realms tend to war against each other. This is why we have questions and why we must renew our minds to the truth by meditating on God's Word, because in the natural realm, this made absolutely no sense to Mary. How can she become pregnant as a virgin? How many times have we also asked,

"How? How are You going to do that, God? How in the world can this be done? How is it even possible?"

Mary was not rebuked for her question; she was simply given an answer. One of the main reasons Jesus came was to give us answers to life's difficult questions. Gabriel reminds us that there is an answer that God's people can live by, one that is truly trustworthy, which is this: the more time we spend in God's presence, the fewer questions we will struggle with, and the easier answers will flow. Spending time in His presence and in His Word causes us to know He is absolutely trustworthy and what He says will work.

From the presence of God, Gabriel reveals what all humankind needs to hear. It's so simple, yet liberating and hope-filled—*God knows how.* He knows how to untangle the perplexities of life. He knows how to solve mysteries that confound us. He knows how to activate a miracle that changes everything. He knows how to heal us of sickness and disease. With humans, it may be impossible, but with God, all things are possible.

Can you imagine the thoughts and fears that must have initially churned inside of Mary? The fear of what people would think, the fear for her very life. In those times, you could be stoned to death for becoming pregnant outside of marriage. The fear of what would happen to her body; she had never been pregnant before. What does being pregnant with Heaven's child mean? How does that work? The fear of not being able to take care of the baby; what young lady wouldn't have felt the weight of that responsibility, of being the mother of God's Son? Not to mention the fear of what Joseph would think, or her parents, grandparents, and friends. What does this do to the wedding plans? Will Joseph cancel them? How is she going to explain this? No wonder the Scriptures say that Mary was troubled at Gabriel's words. She had to have been thinking, *What kind of talk is this?*

Mary found herself in an unbelievable situation, and if ever something appeared impossible, this was it. How can this be? It was all out of her hands. She couldn't make this happen. Most of us have faced situations that were out of our hands, that we couldn't control. God was going to do something that involved Mary. He made promises that were going to happen to her and there was nothing she could do to bring them to pass. It was up to God. All Mary could do was submit to His plan and trust Him.

This is one of the greatest examples of faith in all the Scriptures. Even with questions swirling in Mary's mind, doubt clawing at her senses, fear churning in her heart, unbelief pushing for control of her thinking, with hopelessness gripping her mind and thoughts tormenting her, this young lady stilled herself and made her final statement to Gabriel, *"May it be done to me according to your word"* (Luke 1:38 NASB).

What incredible faith that took. Mary believed something that had never happened *would* happen. Her heart declared, "I believe Your Word. I trust Your promise to me." Luke 1:38, New Living Translation says, *"I am the*

Lord's servant. May everything you have said about me come true." Mary was stating, This is not possible, but with You, God, it is possible." Many today have difficulty trusting, even when they hear testimony after testimony of things God has done. Mary takes it to another level. Although this was something that had never been done, she trusted God.

Many of us have experienced situations in our own lives that provoke us to wonder, *How? How can this be? How can this work out? How can this change?* And like Mary, we think, "I didn't expect this, and I can't do anything about it." A woman at our church recently received a diagnosis that, in the natural, looked hopeless unless she could receive a liver transplant. But God! Just months after receiving this disheartening news, with her health declining, losing weight, and hearing one negative report after another, God stepped into the situation and today she is completely healed. Her own question of "how" turned into a miraculous report.

In my own family, our grandson Jaidin, who was only six years old at the time, underwent what should have been a routine surgery to improve his speech following a cleft palate repair. However, during the surgery, Jaidin suffered a stroke, leaving him unable to swallow anything. He had a feeding tube and was in the hospital for more than a month. *How, God? How will You turn this around? How will you fix this?* Our family clung to a word our daughter, Rachel, Jaidin's mother, had received to "Expect God"—and after seventy-one long days, Jaidin's swallow was healed! Today, all symptoms of the stroke are completely gone!

Life often takes a different turn from what we've planned. It is something we face on this sin-racked, fallen planet. The Christmas story reveals that there are times when life is not going to turn out how we thought. Situations we can't control start controlling us and we need a hope, a strength, a peace that only God can give. There are times when we're doing what we know to do, doing the best we can, and then something comes along that causes us to ask, "What's going on here? This doesn't make sense to my natural mind. How can this be? Is this good? How will my life be changed by this?" We have to come to the place where, like Mary, we admit we cannot handle it on our own, that in our own strength it is impossible.

Many times, I have had a promise from God or I received a prophetic word and I struggled to believe because of what I could see. Often, I have tried with all my heart to believe, but doubt clawed at my senses as I struggled with unbelief, controlling fear, and hopelessness because my eyes saw a situation that I couldn't change. I would be facing a situation I couldn't do anything about, humanly speaking. In light of His promise, I have asked, "How can this be?"

How many times does life give us a scenario, that in light of God's Word, our lack of understanding says, "But how?" How can life become abundant? How can I be healed? How can I survive this? How can I ever be joyful again? How can this mountain move? How can this complicated situation ever change? How can this ever be turned and become a blessing?

The Christmas story reveals a magnificent answer—God knows how.

REFLECTION

Mary heard that answer and it's one we need to hear, as well. It's been tested and proven through the ages—God knows how. He knows how to do what we can't do. He knows how to make happen what we can't make happen. What is impossible with us, He knows how to do. He knows how to do miracles. He knows how to change our lives forever and bring forth new destiny and purpose, just as He did for Mary. He knows how to give victory when we can't see how. He knows how to provide. He knows how to promote. He knows how to restore. He knows how to bless, deliver, save, open doors, protect us, prosper us, and make a way when we can't see a way. Even something that's never been done before, as in Mary's case, He knows how. He's the One who has done a million firsts. God knows how.

DR. TIM SHEETS is an apostle, pastor, and author based in southwestern Ohio. He ministers nationally and internationally at conferences, churches, seminars, and Bible schools. He is a graduate of Christ For the Nations Institute and has a Doctorate of Divinity from Christian Life School of Theology. He is the author of the best-seller *Angel Armies* as well as *Planting the Heavens* and *Heaven Made Real.* His latest book, *The New Era of Glory,* was released by Destiny Image Publishers nationwide January 2019.

Dr. Sheets is the founder of AwakeningNow Prayer Network and travels throughout a ten-state region holding prayer assemblies and establishing 24/7 prayer in local churches. He is also the pastor of Oasis Church in Middletown, Ohio. Dr. Sheets resides with his wife, Carol, in Lebanon, Ohio. They have two children, Rachel (Mark) Shafer, and Joshua (Jessica) Sheets, and seven grandchildren: Madeline, Lily, Jude, Jaidin, Joelle, Sam, and Grace.

THE GLORY
OF FOLLOWING
GOD'S LEAD

by Mike Bickle

The Christmas story is a remarkable narrative of how God used a young girl to partner with Him in bringing His Son to the earth. It is a glorious story that reveals how God leads and how He wants people to respond to His leadership when He is breaking into human history in an historic way. When the angel Gabriel told Mary that she would conceive and bear the Messiah, Mary responded with a heart of willingness and trust in the Lord's leadership. God is looking for this kind of heart response in His people.

As we look at the Christmas story, we should not merely admire the nobility of Mary's calling and choices; Mary's life is a model that can inspire us to respond rightly to God's leadership throughout our lives, especially in seasons when circumstances become difficult.

The angel Gabriel was sent to the small town of Nazareth. He visited Mary, a young virgin, and greeted her saying, *"...Rejoice, highly favored one, the Lord is with you; blessed are you among women!"* (Luke 1:28 NKJV). Can you imagine the angel Gabriel appearing to you and declaring such wonderful things about your life? You would expect that being favored and blessed by God would mean that you would have a life of blessed circumstances with maybe a little difficulty here and there. However, the glorious promises of God that Mary was about to receive would unfold slowly through many surprisingly difficult seasons. Mary would need to hold on to and remember Gabriel's encouraging words throughout her life as she carried the promises of God in her heart.

After greeting Mary, Gabriel told her that she would conceive by the Holy Spirit and bear a Son, Jesus. He revealed to Mary that her Son would be great and would be called the Son of the Highest. Her Son, Jesus, would be given the throne of David and would reign forever. Gabriel was summarizing what Isaiah had prophesied hundreds of years earlier, *"For unto us a Child is born, unto us a Son is given, and the government will be upon His shoulder. And His name will be called Wonderful, Counselor, Mighty God, Everlasting Father, Prince of Peace"* (Isaiah 9:6 NKJV).

126

Mary knew the prophetic Scriptures, and now Gabriel told her that she would bear the Messiah of whom they foretold. Instead of shrinking back in fear or unbelief, Mary responded to these glorious promises with a willing heart for God to do to her as He had said. She believed Him.

Gabriel's initial charge for Mary to "Rejoice" was a practical, pastoral exhortation that she was to engage in for the rest of her life as she carried these promises in her heart. It was not a one-time call of exuberance to explode with joy at the possibility of what was happening. Through the troubles and misunderstandings that Mary would experience, she would continually need to lay hold of the command to rejoice and trust the Lord's good leadership in her life. Choosing to rejoice in God's promises despite hardship would realign Mary's heart repeatedly in the years ahead, strengthening her to persevere and to continue to grow in faith.

THE FAVOR OF GOD

What does a life look like under the favor of God? It is easy to miss some of the unexpected hardships that Mary endured for decades to come. As spoken by the angel Gabriel, Mary conceived by the Holy Spirit. God was with her, but she initially experienced tremendous amounts of shame. After being visited by Gabriel, Mary traveled 100 miles south to Judah and spent over three months with Elizabeth. When Mary returned home to

Nazareth, she was visibly pregnant. This was a serious issue because she had already been engaged to Joseph.

In the ancient world, a broken engagement would require a legal divorce. If she had been with another man, Mary would have been guilty by law to be stoned. Her story was that God made her pregnant. Mary would have seemed like a bold-faced liar or so delusional that it would have been another problem. Her fiancé, Joseph, was deeply troubled, and rumors were spreading throughout her community. More than thirty years later, these same rumors of Mary's fornication were still being passed around in Jerusalem (John 8:41).

Before God stepped in and told him that Mary was telling the truth, Joseph was planning to break off his relationship with her. The Lord was dramatically using Mary, but she experienced intense shame and misunderstanding from those she loved most. Through it all, Mary's heart was growing in love, faith, and humility.

The way that we grow in mature love, faith, and humility is by choosing to trust God again and again in the face of unexpected hardships and the unexpected delay of some of His promises to us. When we are perplexed and want to operate in the flesh but stop and say, "God, I trust Your leadership," we are realigning our hearts with His heart and promises. In believing God's promises and responding with faith and gratitude despite difficulties, we are rejoicing like Mary did. Through this process of realigning our heart, even thousands of times, we slowly grow in love, faith, and humility. Mary did this repeatedly throughout her life, and, as she did, she matured in her love for the Lord and in her confidence in His good leadership.

Toward the end of Mary's pregnancy, she had to make the long, intense journey to Bethlehem with Joseph for the census. After they arrived, she was ready to give birth, but there was no room for them in the inn. She went through the agony of labor in a dirty stable and then had only a manger in which to lay her beloved newborn Son. I would have thought that since the angel Gabriel told Mary that God's favor was upon her and she would bear a Son who would reign forever that the circumstances around His birth would have been a bit easier. Mary had received these great promises and endured the months of intense shame, but now she did not even have a proper place to deliver and care for her Son.

Despite the difficulties and human dynamics that Mary experienced, a series of supernatural events surrounded Jesus' birth. Shortly after Jesus was born, some excited shepherds showed up looking for a baby in a manger. An angel had told them that Christ the Savior had been born and was lying in a manger. The shepherds tell Mary that they saw a host of angels praising God over her Son's birth. Later on, when Mary and Joseph went to dedicate Jesus in Jerusalem, two prophetic witnesses, Simeon and Anna, testified of Jesus' glorious identity. Afterward, wise men from the East brought gifts and came to worship Jesus. After all that Mary had endured since Gabriel's visit, these things confirmed the promises over Jesus' life and encouraged Mary that God was really with her.

UNEXPECTED CHALLENGES

After all of these glorious confirmations of the Lord's promises, I would have expected things to be a bit easier for Mary in the coming years. Although God was moving powerfully in Mary's life, the difficulties, delays, and opportunities for discouragement were not over. Not long after the magi left, an angel visited Joseph in a dream, warning him to flee with his family to Egypt because Herod wanted to kill Jesus. Imagine this. Young Mary had borne the stigma and shame of her pregnancy among her friends and relatives; now she had to temporarily flee with her family to a foreign land because the government sought to destroy her little Boy. Is this what a blessed and favored life looks like? There are sometimes very unexpected challenges in the midst of fully receiving and walking out the Lord's good promises.

Things became even more difficult for Mary down the road. Joseph was still there when Jesus was twelve, but Mary was widowed sometime after that. Matthew 13:55-56 mentions that Jesus had four brothers and several sisters. What does a widowed woman do with seven or eight children in their teens and younger? In addition to experiencing the pain and trauma of losing her husband, Mary would have faced incredible pressure as a widow with so many children.

When Jesus was thirty, He took six weeks off from the carpenter shop to fast and pray in the wilderness. He returned home anointed by the Holy Spirit, and then the whole town He loved and grew up in turned against Him. He was the most reliable young Man and had a phenomenal reputation; however, the elders of the synagogue were enraged by His claim to be the one of whom Isaiah prophesied. They were so angry that they tried to drive Him off a cliff and kill Him (Luke 4:29).

Mary saw how her Son was so badly mistreated by the leaders of His hometown, and she would have needed to realign her heart again and again in faith with the promises of God throughout His ministry. The angel Gabriel had initially told Mary that Jesus would be great (Luke 1:32). She must have struggled wondering why the elders were so against Him.

After Jesus began His ministry, His brothers did not believe Him (John 7:5). In essence, Mary's own children—whom she raised to honor the God of Israel—did not believe in Jesus even as young adults. Mary must have struggled with the spiritual condition of her sons at the time of Jesus' ministry.

Some of His closest friends and family members considered Jesus as mentally unstable because of the things He was saying and doing (Mark 3:21). The top religious leaders in the nation based in Jerusalem concluded that Jesus was demonized and thus was a dangerous cult leader who was deceiving the people (John 7:47; 8:48). Rumors of Jesus' mother's fornication were passed around in their attempt to discredit Him and His ministry (John 8:41). In other words, Jesus' life and ministry did not appear to be "great" as Gabriel promised. By many standards, it seemed to be just the opposite. Again and again, Mary had to believe the promises of God and trust the Lord's good leadership.

A few years later, Mary watched her Son be rejected by the nation and die on a cross. The religious leaders plotted against Jesus, and the Jewish crowds cried out for Barabbas. Jesus' three and a half years of ministry appeared to have little fruit. He had healed many thousands, but only 120 people believed in Him enough to make it to the prayer meeting in the Upper Room after His resurrection (Acts 1:15).

Mary endured unexpected pain and misunderstanding as she partnered with God and trusted His leadership in her life. Now, her Son's earthly ministry came to an end and He was rejected by the nation rather than exalted as king. The promises were long in coming and it seemed impossible for them to be fulfilled. However, Mary had trusted God from the beginning, and she persevered in trust by the grace of God even here.

THE FULFILLMENT IS YET TO COME

Mary only saw a partial fulfillment of the promises during her lifetime. She conceived by the Holy Spirit and brought forth the Son of God into the world according to the word of the Lord given through Gabriel. However, Gabriel also told Mary that her Son would be great and reign forever. While Jesus was on the earth, He was despised by many and rejected by His brothers, His hometown, and the top political and spiritual leaders of His nation. He suffered and died to bring salvation to sinners before He was raised in glory. The complete fulfillment of the promises over His life will not be until the age to come. A day is coming when He will be seen by all as great in love, power, and mercy. Mary would have seen a glimpse of this during the revivals of the early church, but the fullness is yet future.

Mary's life is a picture of the right heart response to the leadership of God. When she did not fully understand, she trusted God's leadership over and over again. When it seemed to cost her everything, Mary still said, *"Let it be to me according to your word"* (Luke 1:38 NKJV). Mary's trust in God and her willingness to be used by Him and to rejoice in Him was not a one-time response. It was her way of life. She signed up time and time again through the difficulties. She trusted God and repeatedly realigned her heart with God's word.

Rather than give up when things got hard, Mary persevered with joy by the grace of God.

The way that God led and used Mary reflects His perfect leadership. The fulfillment of God's promises is often delayed and released in stages in a context of difficulty to cause us to cling to Him in a way that helps us grow in love, faith, and humility. Being used by God to change history is not the same as being mature in love. God called Mary and then brought her on a journey to grow in greater love. God unfolds His purposes in a hostile world and uses the adversity to bring forth His people in mature love, humility, and partnership.

INVITATION

God desires to partner with those who will trust Him through everything and continually say yes to Him without quitting. Like Mary, we need to realign our hearts in agreement with the promises of God and trust His leadership even in difficulties. God's promises are still real when delay and adversity come; the Lord uses these things for our good (Romans 8:28). When we choose to rejoice, hold on to the promises, and trust God through the challenges, He releases grace and empowers us to persevere with joy and grow in love. If we do our part and respond to Him with a willing heart, God will do His part and impart abundant grace.

MIKE BICKLE is the director of the International House of Prayer, an evangelical missions organization based on 24/7 prayer with worship. He is also the founder of International House of Prayer University, which includes full-time ministry, music, and media schools.

Mike is the author of several books, including *Growing in Prayer, Passion for Jesus, God's Answer to the Growing Crisis, Growing in the Prophetic,* and *Prayers to Strengthen Your Inner Man.* Mike's teaching emphasizes growing in passion for Jesus through intimacy with God, doing evangelism and missions work from the place of night-and-day prayer, and the end times. Mike and his wife, Diane, have two married sons and six grandchildren.

GOD'S FRIENDS HAVE A FRONT ROW SEAT TO HIS APPEARING

by Larry Sparks

There is a dimension of intimacy and relationship reserved especially for the friends of God. It's available to "whosoever," but it's extremely exclusive. Everyone is invited into this place, but not everyone accepts the invitation. This realm is called the *Counsel of the Lord*.

FRIENDS HAVE A PLACE IN HIS COUNSEL

The Counsel of the Lord is a spiritual realm where your conversations with God go to another level. It's beyond supplying Heaven with requests and petitions, although we never graduate from offering those up to the Lord. We always need Him and His help, desperately! However, the Counsel of the Lord is not a place of petition; it's a place of intimacy and exchange between friends. It's a place where your heart collides with His, and His words become yours.

Jesus described this place when He said,

> *No longer do I call you servants, for the servant does not know what his master is doing; but* **I have called you friends,** *for all that I have heard from my Father I have made known to you* (John 15:15).

We are still servants of the King; that identity has not been revoked. However, an upgrade has taken place. We are both servants *and* intimates. In relation to Advent and Christmas, it was the friends of God who had a front seat to His arrival. So few were present for His birth. Yet, such has been the case with every move of God on earth. He's usually welcomed by the few faithful friends of God who had their ears pressed into Heaven, waiting for *His* cues.

It's not that only a few friends are invited; *all* are welcome! It's just usually the few who accept the invitation to actually live as the friends of God. Will you receive this invitation this Christmas? It's available!

There are two individuals mentioned in the Christmas story who are not often preached or taught about—Anna and Simeon. While they seemingly play smaller roles in the narrative of Jesus' birth, they are both there, front and center. They were ready for His advent in the midst of a culture that wasn't prepared. How was this possible? I believe these two people functioned in the Counsel of the Lord.

SNEAK PREVIEWS

God gives sneak previews of coming attractions through the prophetic.

> *Indeed, the Sovereign Lord never does anything until he reveals his plans to his servants the prophets* (Amos 3:7 NLT).

While this remains true, I would also suggest that all believers are prophetic and are thus able to recognize what the Holy Spirit is doing. Jesus Himself told us that the Spirit will *"guide you into all the truth, for he will not speak on his own authority, but whatever he hears he will speak, and he will declare to you the things that are to come"* (John 16:13). This is prophetic language for sure. Furthermore, the apostle Paul encourages all believers to earnestly desire the supernatural gifts of the Spirit, *"especially the ability to prophesy"* (1 Corinthians 14:1 NLT).

While there are those who occupy the office of a prophet today, it's also possible for all followers of Jesus who are indwelt by the Spirit to recognize what God is saying and doing. We all have access to the same anointing that Anna and Simeon walked in. Will we walk in it?

SIMEON: A PROPHETIC FRONT ROW SEAT TO THE MOVE OF GOD

As they came to the temple to fulfill this requirement, an elderly man was there waiting—a resident of Jerusalem whose name was Simeon. He was a very good man, a lover of God who kept himself pure, and the Spirit of holiness rested upon him. Simeon believed in the imminent appearing of the one called "The Refreshing of Israel." For the Holy Spirit had revealed to him that he would not see death before he saw the Messiah, the Anointed One of God. For this reason the Holy Spirit had moved him to be in the temple court at the very moment Jesus' parents entered to fulfill the requirement of the sacrifice (Luke 2:25-27 TPT).

Simeon was in the temple...waiting. It was as if he anticipated this moment. But how? How could Simeon be so ready for Jesus, while so many others seemed to be in the dark concerning His coming? Surely there were other lovers of God who kept themselves pure living in the neighborhood at that time. Did that qualify him to be on the frontlines for this epoch season?

Scripture tells us that Simeon believed in the imminent appearing of *"the one called 'The Refreshing of Israel'"* because the Holy Spirit revealed this to him. When we read between the lines of this account, we see a man who lived intimately connected to the Spirit of God. He was a friend of Yahweh.

Luke 2:27 in the English Standard Version of the Bible says it all concerning Simeon's relationship with God: *"And he* [Simeon] *came in the Spirit into the temple, and when the parents brought in the child Jesus, to do for him according to the custom of the Law."* Simeon lived *in the Spirit,* vitally connected to God. I have a sneaking suspicion that it would have been difficult to discern where God ended and Simeon began, in terms of how connected this man was with the Master.

Intimacy with God will always prophetically position you to have the front seat on the move of the Spirit. How? You know His nature, His character, and His ways; thus, you can trace His movement, even before others. This doesn't give license for spiritual pride or superiority. Far from it. When we see God is moving, it's the great joy of our lives to announce it, celebrate it, and partner with it. This was Simeon!

Anna: Prayer Is Always the Posture

Anna, a prophet, was also there in the Temple. She was the daughter of Phanuel from the tribe of Asher, and she was very old. Her husband died when they had been married only seven years. Then she lived as a widow to the age of eighty-four. She never left the Temple but stayed there day and night, worshiping God with fasting and prayer. She came along just as Simeon was talking with Mary and Joseph, and she began praising

God. She talked about the child to everyone who had been waiting expectantly for God to rescue Jerusalem (Luke 2:36-38 NLT).

Even though Anna was a prophetess, I don't want to focus on that office or function. I want to explore what she was actually doing in the temple that postured her to be ready for a divine appointment with Jesus and His family. I want to make her more relevant to you! I know the text says that she never left the physical temple, remaining there day and night worshiping God with fasting and prayer. We no longer need to go to a specific place in order to worship God and enjoy His presence. In that era, prior to the redemptive work of the Messiah, the temple was the place of Presence, the place of intimacy, the place of communion.

Now, *you* are the temple of Presence, intimacy, and communion! You can follow Anna's example wherever you are, praying without ceasing (see 1 Thessalonians 5:17), continually singing praises to the Lord (see Ephesians 5:19), and presenting your life as a living sacrifice—the acceptable act of worship (see Romans 12:1). You are a portable prayer and praise meeting. When you live in that posture, your spiritual ears will always be bent toward Heaven and you'll always have that front seat to what God is doing.

Now it's time for you *to enter His counsel, seek His heart, discover His plans,* and *take your place.*

Anna and Simeon were intimates of the Lord. What is the key factor that identifies people as such friends of God? It's what they do with His *heart*. They don't just want spiritual information or intelligence from Him. They don't merely seek breakthrough formulas or blessing strategies. They are not on a quest to appear spiritual, as those who can prophetically hear what God is saying and transmit His word using all of the supernatural eloquence that one can muster. Intimates chase after the very heart of God.

We see a direct connection between this place called the Counsel of the Lord and the plans within God's heart. Psalm 33:11 states, *"The counsel of the Lord stands forever, the plans of his heart to all generations."* Those who have access to His counsel will always have a window of access to know His plans, His intentions, His desires, His motivations. The crowds always want to see His acts and miracles. The masses will always seek Him for what He *does* and what He *offers*. Of course, He does much for us and offers abundance beyond our ability to comprehend. But that's not why we seek Him. That's not what motivated Anna or Simeon. Front-row access to the move of God will always be reserved for His friends.

In the Old Testament, the prophet Jeremiah was speaking against the false prophets of his day. They were not speaking words of the Lord, but rather, speaking forth *"visions of their own minds,"* filling the people with *"vain hopes"* (Jeremiah 23:16). God speaking through Jeremiah asks the following question, *"For who among them has stood in the council of the Lord to see and to hear his word, or who has paid attention to his word and listened?"* (Jeremiah 23:18). God was looking for more than prophets; He was seeking true friends. Catch this: God was looking for those who could do more than simply hear and repeat; He was looking for those who had His heart.

Many claimed then, and claim today, to be speaking words on behalf of God. They might even communicate some information accurately, but if their speech does not transmit both the content and character of God, the prophetic messages are off. *Intimates of God will always represent Him accurately.* I am not interested in just sharing words; I want them to be words from His heart.

God spoke through Jeremiah, lamenting about the prophets of the day: *"But if they had stood in my council, then they would have proclaimed my words to my people..."* (Jeremiah 23:22).

It's a prophetic dimension where you are given ears to hear what the Spirit of God is saying. But it's not enough to simply hear what He is saying; you are called to become a discerner of times and seasons that births the purposes of God into earth through intercession. The Sovereign God who doesn't require a thing from anyone, especially frail humanity, has summoned you into His counsel. He wants to share things with you so you are ready for what He wants to do in your life and on the earth.

REFLECTION AND RESPONSE

Let's live as Anna and Simeon did, intimates and friends of God who ultimately had front-row access to the glorious advent of Messiah Jesus. Such people are always welcome in His counsel, not because they are seeking rewards or riches, but rather, the riches and rewards are wrapped in swaddling clothes, lying in a manger. The greater reward is beholding His glory. It's obvious this was the great quest of both Simeon and Anna because of what the Scriptures reveal.

Upon seeing Jesus, Simeon responds, "Sovereign Lord, now let your servant die in peace, as you have promised. I have seen your salvation" (Luke 2:29-30 NLT). Beholding the Messiah was Simeon's reward. For Anna, the sight of the Messiah caused an eruption of praise: "She came along just as Simeon was talking with Mary and Joseph, and she began praising God. She talked about the child to everyone who had been waiting expectantly for God to rescue Jerusalem" (Luke 2:38 NLT).

The great reward of God's friends is always Himself. And these men and women, sons and daughters, have historically been positioned—often in the most unlikely of places—to have front-row seats to moves of Heaven that have touched and changed the earth. And there was no greater move than what was beheld by the eyes of this man and woman, Simeon and Ana.

BEHOLD THE PREEXISTENT CHRIST

by Kevin Zadai

The Christmas season is a special time to celebrate the birth of our Lord Jesus Christ. We recognize His advent on the earth as God Almighty in bodily form. As a baby, Jesus entered our world with a divine plan and purpose for all humanity. Jesus touched many lives as He walked among us for approximately thirty-three years, healing the sick, casting out demons, raising the dead, and preaching the message of the Kingdom.

However, behind the scenes, did you ever think about the activities of Heaven that were happening in the planning stages that led to the fulfillment of this event that we call Christmas?

In eternity, God has established His throne in Heaven. He is from a timeless realm that we call the spirit realm, and therefore He has no limitations. God's limitless power is unlike the limitations of human beings. It is hard to comprehend the fact that the Lord has always existed and will continue to exist forever. Due to His eternal existence, the Lord's throne has always been and will still be, the seat of power for all creation. The Father, the Son, and the Holy Spirit were all together in a preexistent state in glory long before humans ever existed. Even holy angels existed before there was a human race. The Almighty is quoted in Job as asking:

> *Where were you when I laid the foundations of the earth? Tell Me, if you have an understanding. Who determined its measurements? Surely you know! Or who stretched the line upon it? To what were its foundations fastened? Or who laid its cornerstone, when the **morning stars** sang together, and all the **sons of God** [angels] shouted for joy?* (Job 38:4-7 NKJV)

The angels in Heaven have been dispatched to serve with and for us in this last great move of His Spirit on the earth! Angels were created to implement God's plan for each one of us. Just as they were there to announce the glorious birth of Jesus (see Luke 2). They are part of the preexisting Kingdom of God and therefore work with us to help fulfill all that God has planned for us while on this earth.

To fully comprehend the power that angels have, we must accept the fact that God has an eternal existence and Kingdom that is above all. In God Almighty's pre-existence, He established a throne, and it's from His powerful throne that He rules the universe with great authority. The purpose of angels has always been to fulfill God's redemptive plans for each of us. The Lord establishes those plans from His throne, which is the seat of authority in the heavenlies.

Because of God's foreknowledge, He knew that when He created man and woman that they would choose to disobey and eat of the tree of the knowledge of good and evil and fall away. The Trinity met and decided before-hand to provide redemption for humanity through Jesus Christ. Jesus was chosen to be born of a woman to pur-chase humans in their fallen state:

> *For to us a Child shall be born, to us a Son shall be given; and the government shall be upon His shoulder, and His name shall be called Wonderful Counselor, Mighty God, Everlasting Father, Prince of Peace. There shall be no end to the increase of His government and of peace, [He shall rule] on the throne of David and over his kingdom, to establish it and to uphold it with justice and righteousness from that time forward and forevermore. The zeal of the Lord of hosts will accomplish this* (Isaiah 9:6-7 Amplified Bible).

God has a government of righteousness and justice that invites all whom He has created to serve Him and be under His loving care. The angels understand the authority that God has over all of creation; but human-kind, in the fallen state, did not understand the need for a Savior. No one will ever be able to usurp or over-take God's authority and drive Him out of the seat of His power. Angels have been sent throughout the universe to enforce God's rule, and they will continue until what the apostle Paul spoke of in the Book of Romans comes to pass:

> *I consider that the sufferings of this present time are not worthy to be compared with the glory which shall be revealed in us. For the earnest expectation of the* **creation eagerly waits for the revealing of the sons of God** (Romans 8:18-19 NKJV).

We can see as Christians that we are to yield to the Holy Spirit and allow His powerful work to usher us into the glory of the Father. Jesus shared in this glory with the Father before the universes were lit up with light. Jesus said, *"So my Father, restore me back to the glory that we shared together when we were face-to-face before the universe was created"* (John 17:5 TPT). We are to share in the same glory as sons and daughters of God when that day comes because that eternal weight of glory is in us.

The King James Version of the Bible says in Second Corinthians 4:17, *"For our light affliction, which is but for a moment, worketh for us a far more exceeding and eternal weight of glory."* The glory of the Father that was upon Jesus will be manifested in us in the latter days as the body of Christ is built up in the unity of the faith.

God's plan was that Jesus would replace the sacrifices of the Old Testament law. Jesus, through His obedience, has taken our relationship with the Father to the original intimate level that was intended from the beginning, before the fall.

> *When Jesus the Messiah came into the world he said, "Since your ultimate desire was not another animal sacrifice, you have clothed me with a body that I might offer myself instead! Multiple burnt offerings and sin-offerings cannot satisfy your justice." So I said to you, "God—I will be the One to go and do your will, to fulfill all that is written of me in your Word!"* (Hebrews 10:5-7 TPT)

This salvation was planned for us by the Trinity from the foundation of the world because of God's love for us (see Revelation 13:8). We can rest assured that God's plan for humankind will be accomplished if we will acknowledge what He has done for us and agree to participate in the divine nature as mentioned in Second Peter. We have the ability through powerful and effective promises of the Word of God, to encounter the glory of God in our lives.

> *As a result of this, he has given you magnificent promises that are beyond all price, so that through the power of these tremendous promises you can experience partnership with the divine nature, by which you have escaped the corrupt desires that are of the world* (2 Peter 1:4 TPT).

The apostle Peter says that we have a partnership in the divine nature of God, as we have through Him, escaped the corruption in this world. All of this is because Jesus, the Son of God and the Son of Man, came to visit us beginning in a humble manger. He grew up and walked among us as an example of how to live in the power of the Spirit. Finally, after suffering and dying on the Cross, Jesus finished His conquest with a mighty ascension to the right hand of the Father. He is absolutely the victorious Son of God!

ARE YOU READY?

Are you ready to walk in this supernatural way of life that was purchased at a great price through redemption? God has plans for you to walk in great authority and power.

Even our very words should not reflect human wisdom, but we should have power and demonstration in the Holy Spirit in everything we do (see 1 Corinthians 2:4). During this Christmas season, let us reflect on what God has accomplished for us in this life and planned out for us before the universe was first lit up. He truly loves humanity and has demonstrated that love through His Son, Jesus Christ. Jesus will receive His reward for redeeming us on that day when we all stand before Him and worship Him as the Lamb who was slain before the foundation of the world (see Revelation 13:8).

Jesus is your *Victorious Warrior!* He has paved the way for you to encounter the glory of the Father. As you reflect on what Christmas means to us during this season, be reminded that He came for you and wants all of us to join Him in the holy celebration of His birth. However, there is so much more that He has accomplished for you. In His preexistent state, Jesus wrote a book about you before you were born and planned out all your days (see Psalm 139:16). Right now, angels are reading what is written in your book and are commanded by the Lord to help you fulfill all that has been written about you.

The Lord is saying to you now by the Holy Spirit, that today, you can walk in the power of Jesus' life on this earth. The same mighty power that raised Jesus from the dead has been given to you (see Romans 8:11). Although He was laid in a humble manger, in a mighty display of power He will return again one day as the Lion of the tribe of Judah.

> [We are writing] about the Word of Life [in] Him Who existed from the beginning, Whom we have heard, Whom we have seen with our [own] eyes, Whom we have gazed upon [for ourselves] and have touched with our [own] hands. And the Life [an aspect of His being] was revealed (made manifest, demonstrated), and we saw [as eyewitnesses] and are testifying to and declare to you the Life, the eternal Life [in Him] Who already existed with the Father and Who [actually] was made visible (was revealed) to us [His followers]. What we have seen and [ourselves] heard, we are also telling you, so that you too may [d]realize and enjoy fellowship as partners and partakers with us. And [this] fellowship that we have

[which is a distinguishing mark of Christians] is with
the Father and with His Son Jesus Christ (the Messiah)
(1 John 1:1-3 Amplified Bible, Classic Edition).

We are destined to encounter His glory in the deep, intimate fellowship that comes from holy worship. The world doesn't know Him as His children do. As you worship the King of kings this Christmas, pray that you may have a spirit of wisdom and revelation come upon you. Believe that in this season, you will encounter the revelation of the glory that is in the Father and shared with the Son, and now with His children through salvation.

I have personally beheld Jesus in glory, and this encounter has forever changed me. He is so worthy and yet He wants us to be with Him in that same glory with the Father. At this moment, angels are worshipping Him, and the saints who have gone before us fall down and adore Him.

Be encouraged as you celebrate His coming and know that your worship is accepted. As you reach out to others, see that you are the Savior's hand of compassion to a lost and dying world who desperately needs the revelation of God's love.

REFLECTION

Here's what I feel the Spirit of the Lord is saying to
you in this season: "Though I have come to you as a
humble servant in a manger, I left you as a triumphant

King and gave you full rights to the earth. I have sent you the mighty Holy Spirit to empower you in word and in deed. In My name, take back what satan has stolen from humanity. Drive satan out by healing the sick, raising the dead, and preaching the Good News to everyone. I will come back for you, and you shall be with Me forever. You shall rule and reign as kings with Me, forever. I have made you priests and kings of the Most High God, and you shall see great victory. Nothing shall be impossible to you for I am with you as a Mighty Warrior."

KEVIN ZADAI, THD, is dedicated to training Christians to live and operate in two realms at once—the supernatural and the natural. Called to ministry at age ten, he attended Central Bible College in Springfield, Missouri, where he received a Bachelor's degree in Theology. Later, Kevin received training in missions at Rhema Bible College. At age thirty-one, during a routine surgery, he found himself on the "other side of the veil" with Jesus in a heavenly visitation that forever marked his life. This encounter ushered his ministry into new dimensions of power, activation, and impartation. Kevin is retired after being employed by Southwest Airlines for twenty-nine years; he and his wife, Kathi, reside in New Orleans,

Louisiana, and are ordained by Dr. Jesse and Dr. Cathy
Duplantis.

A TIME OF PREPARATION

by Norman Benz

nd then there was silence. Four hundred years of silence. No word from God through the prophets, priests, or kings. Just silence! From the days of Malachi to the beginning of the Gospel according to Matthew—nothing.

It must have been ingrained in the spirit of the people in Israel to have a great hope and expectancy—surely the Messiah will come. Over seven hundred years earlier, the prophet Isaiah proclaimed that God was coming in a very special manner:

Therefore the Lord himself will give you a sign: The virgin will be with child and will give birth to a son, and will call him Immanuel. …Nevertheless, there will be no more gloom for those who were in distress. …For to us a child is born, to us a son is given, and the government will be on his shoulders. And he will be called Wonderful Counselor, Mighty God, Everlasting Father, Prince of Peace (Isaiah 7:14; 9:1,6 New International Version).

Then everything changed. It was the fulfillment of prophecy. The future was changed. The Messiah has come. It was unbelievable. God became human. Jesus was the Christ, the Son of Man, but yet, He was the Son of God. Isaiah said, *"God is with us, Immanuel."*

The Holy Spirit hovered over Mary and *"she was found to be with child"* (Matthew 1:18).

In Christendom today, many churches observe the season of Advent. Advent means "coming." It points to the birth of Jesus our Messiah, but also a time of preparing for His coming. The longing for the Messiah that was planted deep in the Jewish faith and people caused them to know that something better was coming.

Advent is a time of preparation. In our personal moments, it is a time for seeking the presence of God in our world and watching for the *"restoration of all things"* (Matthew 19:28 TPT). In our Advent preparations for His coming, a powerful truth emerges: Jesus the Christ does not save from a distance. He is intimately involved with us. He walks among us. He dwells with us. He went to the disenfranchised and the unwanted. He identifies with the oppressed and the excluded. God became flesh (John 1:14); He became poor (2 Corinthians 8:9); He became "God with us."

For years I have celebrated Advent with our congregation, and it looks something like this:

The four Sundays before Christmas are known as the four Sundays of Advent. While there are variations within the tradition, these Sundays are known as hope, love, joy, and peace.

The Advent Candle Wreath is a circle reminding us of the perfection and eternity of God also indicating His everlasting love. The evergreen branches are symbolic of life. The three purple candles represent the royalty of Christ and the penitence of humankind. Only the shepherd's candle is a different color, rose, signifying joy.

The first Sunday of Advent is the Sunday of hope. Our hope is in God, and in His Son, Jesus Christ. He is the One appointed by God to be Judge of all things. He is the One through whom God has promised to save and redeem His people. We light this candle to remind us that He is our Hope and the Hope of the world. We thank God for the promises He has made to us and for the light He has brought into the world. There is hope in our hearts for the Messiah will lead us out of dark and difficult times. This candle of hope reminds us that Jesus is sent to us because of God's great love.

The second Sunday of Advent is the Sunday of love. Jesus shows us God's perfect love. He is God's perfect love in human form. Those who believe in Him and live in Him live in love. Love transforms and perfects all things. It never ends. We light this candle to remind us that God is love. We thank God for the hope He gives us, for the peace He bestows, for the joy He pours into our hearts, and for the love that redeems us and shows us the way.

The third Sunday of Advent is the Sunday of joy. Our joy is in God and in His Son, Jesus Christ. Like peace, joy is a gift from God. It overtakes us and fills us when we remember what God has done and what He has promised to do. We light this rose-colored candle to remind us that Christ came, and is coming, so that all people might have a rich and abundant life. We thank God for the hope He gives us, for the peace He bestows, and for the joy He pours into our hearts. This candle reminds us of the angels' great news told to the shepherds.

The fourth Sunday of Advent is the Sunday of peace and reminds us that Jesus came to bring peace and goodwill. Our peace is found in God and in His Son, Jesus Christ. John the Baptist, and all the prophets remind us that to receive peace we must be prepared for it. We light this candle to remind us that Christ is the Prince of Peace, the One promised from the beginning of the world. We thank God for the hope He gives us and for the peace He bestows.

During the Christmas Eve service, there is a fifth candle in the middle of the wreath—a large white candle. This candle represents that Christ the Messiah has come. On this night, we light the Christ Candle—He has come. This is the ultimate purpose for our Advent preparations—the baby Jesus.

The failure of the people of biblical history to represent God points to the necessity of the advent of Christ. Prepare your heart for something new. Isaiah 43:19 (NLT) says, *"I am about to do something new. See, I have already begun! Do you not see it? I will make a pathway through the wilderness. I will create rivers in the dry wasteland."*

PRAYER

Holy Spirit, put a longing in our hearts for more of Jesus. Holy Spirit, do a creative work through us. Breathe on us, Holy Spirit. Hover over us. Give us wisdom and revelation. Create within us a great hope. Dispel disappointment. Bring new life and invigorate us with a renewed resolve.

NORMAN BENZ has been in the pastoral ministry for fifty years. He and his wife Judy are the co-founding pastors of Covenant Centre International in 1991 in Palm Beach Gardens, Florida. Since their church received a powerful outpouring from the Holy Spirit in 1997 their lives and Covenant have been transformed as they continue to keep the Holy Spirit fire burning. Norman holds a M.Ed. (Florida Atlantic University), M. Div. (Church of God School of Theology), and received his D. Min. from Reformed Theological Seminary. His dissertation project was *Revival: When the Holy Spirit Comes Down*. He and Judy continue to be a catalyst for Holy Spirit.

THE CALL TO WORSHIP THE KING

by Pat Schatzline

Go back with me two thousand years. The heavens had been silent for hundreds of years. The world was asleep, but the heavens were roaring. I imagine that all of Heaven was standing at attention as when an Olympic torchbearer enters the stadium to light the giant ring of fire. Tonight was the night that thousands of years of prophecy would begin to unfold. An earthly king would have expected a grand coronation. People from all over would come to pay their respects. There would be parties, banquets, and pomp galore if this was an earthly king.

No, instead this King would enter into humanity in the humblest of fashions. He would not arrive on a white horse or fine chariot. He would simply be birthed in a lean-to shed where animals stood when feeding time arrived and where manure odor filled the air. This was befitting to the fact that our King would also become our Lamb. Humanity needed a lamb; a Savior who would save the people of the world from themselves. The Bible says that the blood of animals couldn't keep covering our sin (Hebrews 10:4-5). There had to be an ultimate sacrifice. Humankind needed Someone to do away with the old and establish a new life (Hebrews 10:9).

The final altar had to be built. Many prophets foretold that a Messiah would come and rescue the people, including the oldest book of the Bible, Job. A promise is declared in Job 19:25, *"For I know that my Redeemer lives, and at the last he will stand upon the earth."* The word "redeemer," or *ga'al* in Hebrew, means the avenger or to ransom or purchase with blood.[1] The prophet Isaiah gave us the best clues about the coming Messiah:

> *Therefore the Lord himself will give you a sign. Behold, the virgin shall conceive and bear a son, and shall call his name Immanuel. …For to us a child is born, to us a son is given; and the government shall be upon his shoulder, and his name shall be called Wonderful Counselor, Mighty God, Everlasting Father, Prince of Peace. …He was oppressed, and he was afflicted, yet he opened not his mouth; like a lamb that is led to the*

slaughter, and like a sheep before its shearers is silent,
so he opened not his mouth (Isaiah 7:14; 9:6; 53:7).

For thousands of years humanity waited for a Savior. Finally, He arrived! It was the ultimate altar call the night He was born! The Lamb is named Jesus! Now Heaven was giving the very altar call!

I imagine it was a cold, dark night with the wind howling across the plains of Israel. Imagine that the shepherds were settling in for a simple night of very little excitement except the sound of bleating sheep and the rustling of the wind. Somewhere between dawn and twilight, the sky erupted in praise! Then suddenly, their sensory vision was overwhelmed with an explosion in the sky above. God always knows how to make a grand entrance! This was the first altar call invitation!

An angel of the Lord appeared to them, and the glory of the Lord shone around them, and they were filled with great fear. And the angel said to them, "Fear not, for behold, I bring you good news of great joy that will be for all the people. For unto you is born this day in the city of David a Savior, who is Christ the Lord. And this will be a sign for you: you will find a baby wrapped in swaddling cloths and lying in a manger" (Luke 2:9-12).

A heavenly host suddenly cried out in jubilee that the King had been born. There had been no celebration planned in advance of this King's appearance; instead, God would have to awaken some lowly shepherds to provide the welcome party for the King of Israel and the King of our souls.

It was the shepherds who welcomed the newborn King! We shouldn't be shocked. God always uses shepherds. Look at Moses and David, they were shepherding when their lives were interrupted. "Shepherds" in the Greek is *poy-mane,* meaning "a herdsman, overseer to which ones' care has been committed." We are all shepherds! God wants to interrupt the shepherds—you and me! He wants to interrupt the ones He trusts with the care of others. We are called to be shepherds to those around us. But first we must awaken!

Christmas must be a reminder to us not of just a seasonal celebration, parties, elves, trees, wreaths, lights, family gatherings, decorations, and Santa, it is a holy reminder that we are called to worship. This will mean shutting down the hustle and bustle of gift hunting and tradition and first finding a place to call our home to worship once again.

There are four things concerning the shepherds that were interrupted on that glorious night by the song of the angels that I want to share with you today! Four things you must understand about these shepherds that God chose to awaken that incredible and historic night that speak to us still today.

1. Shepherds are always on duty!

Luke 2:8 (NKJV) says, *"There were in the same country shepherds living out in the fields, keeping watch over their flock at night."* Here they were, content living in monotony—they had no idea what was about to happen. They would be part of the greatest worship service of all time. What made them so special is that God knew they would be obedient. God knew they would handle the message. These were not normal shepherds. These were Near Eastern shepherds. The task of a Near Eastern shepherd was to watch for enemies trying to attack the sheep, to defend the sheep from attackers, to heal the wounded and sick sheep, to find and save lost or trapped sheep, and to love them, sharing their lives and so earning their trust. Like shepherds, most of all we must keep the enemy away. *"Be sober-minded; be watchful. Your adversary the devil prowls around like a roaring lion, seeking someone to devour"* (1 Peter 5:8). We must be ready to handle the message and be obedient to His calling.

2. The shepherds realized their time had come for their mission!

They were awakened from the monotony of life—peace and favor were here! Luke 2:15 says, *"When the angels went away from them into heaven, the shepherds said to one another, 'Let us go over to Bethlehem and see this thing that has happened, which the Lord has made known to us.'"* I can see them sharing with each other as they walked along, "Dude, nobody is going to believe this." There was such an excitement; they knew they had been visited by God. They were probably running. They were probably weeping—these lowly shepherds were the first evangelists!

God chooses the simple things to confound the wise. He chose the watchers of the lambs! These shepherds were going to find the Head Shepherd. First Peter 2:25 says, *"For you were straying like sheep, but have now returned to the Shepherd and Overseer of your souls."* Mom and Dad, you are the watchers of the lambs! All of us have a mission! We are all called to be shepherds! The shepherds understood they were on a mission. Luke 2:16-18 says, *"And they went with haste and found Mary and Joseph, and the baby lying in a manger. And when they saw it, they made known the saying that had been told them concerning this child. And all who heard it wondered at what the shepherds told them."* I declare that regardless of your past, God is not done with you. It is time to make the dash on your tombstone count. Your mission is not complete. It is never too late to become what God had planned for you to be all along.

3. WHEN THE SHEPHERD SHOWS UP EVERYTHING IS OKAY!

Luke 2:20, *"The shepherds returned, glorifying and praising God for all they had heard and seen, as it had been told them."* I bet when they showed up at the manger scene Mary knew everything was going to be okay. Luke 2:19 tells us, *"But Mary treasured up all these things and pondered them in her heart."* We need to have some shepherds show up in this generation! Shepherds who will proclaim to this generation that there is a Savior, a Healer, a Deliverer! These shepherds were the ones who allowed Mary to sit back and think, *Everything is going to be okay.* God proved Himself through the shepherds. He is looking for shepherds through whom He can prove Himself today.

4. Shepherds point the way!

Today let God awaken the shepherds to the Great Shepherd! First Peter 5:1-4 says, *"So I exhort the elders among you, as a fellow elder and a witness of the sufferings of Christ, as well as a partaker in the glory that is going to be revealed: shepherd the flock of God that is among you, exercising oversight, not under compulsion, but willingly, as God would have you; not for shameful gain, but eagerly; not domineering over those in your charge, but being examples to the flock. And when the chief Shepherd appears, you will receive the unfading crown of glory."* The enemy wants to destroy the shepherds, but the angels will awaken you! You are a shepherd and you are called and have influence— use that influence to share with others about the Great Shepherd! Regardless of whether or not you have failed badly in the past or made mistakes that try to keep you in prison, you must start new again. Oswald Chambers once said, "Leave the broken, irreversible past in God's hands, and step out into the invincible future with Him." Today is a new day.

BE THE VOICE THAT INTERRUPTS CHRISTMAS

God is calling us to awaken, we are the shepherds! This Christmas season, I encourage you to look for God-interruptions and allow Him to use you as a voice of life, wisdom, and comfort to others, pointing them in the direction of the Great Shepherd! Several years ago, we found ourselves on the end of a gift hang-over. What do I mean? We would prepare for weeks for Christmas morning only to be left with nice new items, but something was lacking. I felt stirred that there had to be more.

So, we decided to always have communion as a family on Christmas Eve. Then God stirred my heart to take it another step. He reminded me that as the head of my family, I am called to lead differently. I asked the Lord how I could be a better shepherd at Christmas. He said to me, "Spend time with Me and I will give you a prophetic word for each of your children and grandchildren. This word will be with them for one year and they will use it as a compass during the year." I did exactly what the Lord had instructed.

Several days before Christmas I now take time to hide away and hear from the Lord. I then write out on a card a word from the Lord for each of my family. Then on Christmas Eve, I hand deliver the messages. This new tradition changed Christmas at our home. This has become the greatest gift exchange for each of us. After we all share the word out loud with the rest of the family, we come into agreement, take communion, and have a time of worship together.

I challenge every person reading this to be the prophet in your home. Parents, if we do not declare our children's future, then the enemy will try to mark their past. Be the voice of truth, love, and reason. My family will often refer back to the word that was written for them on Christmas throughout the following year. They are astonished when something that had been written from the Lord takes place. They will call and say, "Dad, it is exactly what you wrote from the Lord." The greatest heritage I can leave my family is not more presents or toys, but obedience to the voice of God. We live in a time when truth is the new hate-speech. Be the voice of truth. Be the one who declares that God has free reign in your home.

Trust in the Lord with all your heart, and do not lean on your own understanding. In all your ways acknowledge him, and he will make straight your paths (Proverbs 3:5-6).

REFLECTION

This night changed everything!

This opening of the sky would lead to the tearing in two of a veil (Matthew 27:51).

This child wrapped in swaddling clothes would someday be a Savior naked before humankind (Matthew 27:28-30) who would set the world ablaze.

This cry of a baby Lamb would someday lead to the roar of a mighty Lion.

This innocent little Gift from Heaven would become the doorway to God (Hebrews 10:20).

This Son of God put down His glory so that humankind could experience Him in their hearts.

This first altar call in the New Testament would eventually lead to the ultimate altar call at the Cross.

This is what Christmas is about!

PAT and **KAREN SCHATZLINE** are international evangelists and authors who co-lead Remnant Ministries International and the I Am Remnant Movement. They are known for their passion to lead people of all ages into deep encounters with God. They are frequent guests on Christian television and radio shows such as

The Jim Bakker Show, Sid Roth's *It's Supernatural!,* and *Ask Dr. Brown,* as well as on networks such as Daystar, TBN, JCTV, and GOD TV. They have written several books, including: *Why Is God So Mad at Me?; I Am Remnant; Dehydrated; Unqualified;* and *Rebuilding the Altar.*

Karen also leads *The Breathing Room,* an international, biweekly vlog that ministers to thousands. Married since 1990, they make their home in Fort Worth, Texas. Their joy is their daughter, Abby; son, Nate; daughter-in-love, Adrienne; and grandsons, Jackson and Anderson.

ENDNOTES

1. Blue Letter Bible, s.v. "ga'al," https://www.blueletterbible .org/lang/lexicon/lexicon.cfm?t=kjv&strongs=h1350; accessed May 17, 2019.

2. Oswald Chambers, "Yesterday," My Utmost for His Highest, https://utmost.org/yesterday/.

STAND
BEFORE GOD

by Bob Sorge

Epochal transitions in human history have often been navigated by uncommon angelic activity. When, for example, you see that angels made multiple visits to men like Abraham, Jacob, David, Daniel, John, and Paul, you're tipped off that God was changing times and seasons through their lives in historic ways.

The same thing happened at the coming of the Messiah. Both before and after the birth of Christ, angels appeared to several people—Zacharias, Mary, Joseph, and the shepherds. The explosion of angelic activity surrounding the advent of Christ served to underscore how important this event was in the divine calendar. Heaven was interrupting human history.

The coming of Christ was so significant that Gabriel himself—one of Heaven's mightiest angels—was sent to facilitate the narrative. He appeared first to Zacharias, the father of John the Baptist. While Zacharias was offering incense in the temple, Gabriel suddenly stood before him and told him he would soon have a baby boy. His wife, Elizabeth, who had been barren all their marriage, would give birth to a miracle baby.

Zacharias and Elizabeth had wept and prayed for *decades* for a baby. By now, though, they were both elderly and had probably given up hope. But even though they had stopped asking for a baby, God had not forgotten their prayer and He sent Gabriel to announce His answer.

Zacharias' Renewed Wineskin

The years had taken their toll on Zacharias, however. Decades of heartsickness had made his soul hard and crusty. Gabriel's announcement of a miracle pregnancy was just too good to be true. He couldn't believe it. So, he replied to Gabriel, *"How shall I know this? For I am an old man, and my wife is well advanced in years"* (Luke 1:18 NKJV). Gabriel's response was straight to the point.

*I am Gabriel. **I stand in the presence of God,** and I was sent to speak to you and to bring you this good news.*

And behold, you will be silent and unable to speak until the day that these things take place, because you did not believe my words, which will be fulfilled in their time (Luke 1:19-20).

Zacharias was struck mute, not as punishment for his unbelief, as many suppose, but as a way to soften his hardened wineskin. It's almost as though God was thinking, *Zacharias, I need you to father John the Baptist. He needs to be fathered by a man of the Spirit and faith. And that's not who you are right now. We've got only ten months to change you, so this one is going to be intense. Buckle up, I'm going to use muteness to soften your wineskin and make you the kind of spiritual father John will need.*

Being mute traumatized Zacharias and propelled him into a desperate search of God in the Word and prayer. When he was healed around ten months later, he emerged from the restrictions a totally different man. Instead of questioning God and speaking words of unbelief, he broke out in a prophetic litany, declaring the holy purposes of God through John's life.

I can imagine someone exclaiming, "Zacharias! Who are you? We've never seen this version of you before!" That's because he was profoundly changed in those ten months. The prison had accomplished its work.

Gabriel was sent to encounter Zacharias because history was making a massive transition—from the Old Covenant era to the New Covenant era. Gabriel's usual occupation was to stand in the presence of God; but when he had a divine assignment, he would leave the throne room in order to complete the assignment. Once finished, he would return and take up his place of standing before God.

Six months after his Zacharias assignment, Gabriel was once again tapped for a mission. This time, he was sent to Mary to announce that she would conceive the Messiah by the power of the Holy Spirit.

Mary was young and her heart pliable. Unlike Zacharias, she hadn't endured decades of heartsickness and her heart wasn't calcified. When Gabriel announced her imminent pregnancy, Mary believed and simply said, *"Behold the maidservant of the Lord! Let it be to me according to your word"* (Luke 1:38 NKJV).

GABRIEL STANDS BEFORE GOD

Gabriel is mentioned three times in Scripture. The first was when he visited Daniel (Daniel 8:16). The second was almost *six hundred years later* when he appeared to Zacharias (Luke 1:19). The third was *six months later* when he spoke with Mary (Luke 1:26).

That was the busy season.

"So what do you do, Gabriel?" we might ask.

"I stand in the presence of God."

"Yes, we understand that, but what do you do?"

"Actually, I stand in the presence of God."

"Yes, yes, Gabriel, we understand that. But you're such a massive angel. I mean, what does a powerful angel like you *do*?"

Gabriel might say, "That's what I *do*. I stand in the presence of God. I'm spellbound by His limitless glory. All I can do is admire His majestic beauty. It's the most fascinating occupation in the universe. I worship and minister to Him, waiting on Him until He speaks. If He says nothing, I just stand there. When He sends me, I go."

We embrace the same constraints. Everyone born into God's family is part of the Lord's hosts. Like the angels, we stand before the Lord, minister to Him, and stand until He sends us.

You've probably heard the common saying, "Don't just stand there, *do* something!" The Lord inverted that idiom and gave it to me like this: "Don't just do something, *stand* there!" Before I do anything else, my first calling is to stand before Him and minister to Him.

We live in an age when many ministers are more eager to stand before people than before God. We think that authority is to be found by standing before many people, and forget that true authority comes from standing before God. We long to have authority when we stand before people, but who will seek to have authority when they stand before God?

How can we have more authority with people in public than the authority we've cultivated with God in private?

Standing before God is my primary *duty*. But more than that, it's my highest *privilege*.

How could anyone ever promote me when I've already been lifted to the greatest privilege in the universe? I stand before God, exhilarated with the glory of His face, and have the pleasure of giving Him my affection and worship.

THE SERAPHIM STAND BEFORE GOD

No one knows the exhilaration of standing before God better than the seraphim (that was Isaiah's name for them; John called them living creatures). They stand before the throne and gaze upon the glory and splendor of God. They are absolutely riveted by who He is and what He does. Even though they have a tremendous capacity to absorb and retain—signified by their many eyes— they are overwhelmed by what they see and, falling prostrate, they collapse in the presence of His majesty. They can't remain face down for too long, though, because the revelations of God have stirred their appetites and they long for more. Picking themselves up, they stand again before the consuming fire and gaze into the glory of His eternal beauty. They're fascinated, then satisfied, then overwhelmed, and again they throw themselves at the feet of the Ancient of Days. They stand and then collapse; stand and then collapse. For millennia.

And God is no closer to exhausting the revelation of who He is than the day they first beheld Him.

When John was caught up to Heaven, he said he heard voices coming from the throne (Revelation 4:5). Those would be the voices of the four seraphim, for they live inside the throne itself (Revelation 4:6). John doesn't tell us what the seraphim are saying to each other, but I can imagine the conversation sounding something like this:

"Look! Did you just see that?"

"You mean you saw that, too? I thought maybe I was the only one. It's so amazing, I don't even know how to talk about it."

"Yes, I saw that! I have never, in all my life, seen anything so magnificent, so glorious!"

"I feel like I'm seeing Him for the first time!"

"I know what you mean. I thought I was beginning to know Him, but now I realize I haven't even *started* to know the glory and wisdom and power of our Master."

"Holy! Holy! Holy!"

WE ALSO STAND BEFORE GOD

Just like Gabriel and just like the seraphim, we also stand before God and gaze on His glory.

Their capacities help us see what we're called to. For starters, John said the seraphim are *"full of eyes"*

(Revelation 4:6), which speaks of the heft of their mental capacities. They've got the brain power to process data coming to them from hundreds of eyes. These are possibly the most intelligent creatures God ever created. And yet, the smartest creatures in the universe do nothing but stand before Him and gaze on His glory.

Take it from the seraphim, standing before God is the smartest thing you'll ever do.

God created them with that many eyes because He wanted them to be able to function fully in their environment. The Creator deals with humans in the same way. He prepares us for His glory by equipping us with the capacities we need to understand, absorb, and appreciate the glory of who He is.

John called them *"living creatures"* (Revelation 4:6). The thing that struck John was how *alive* they were. In the same way, we come to life when we stand before God.

INVITATION

This Advent, pay attention to all the angels that make appearances in the Christmas story. They'll remind you that you also are a member of the Lord's hosts and have the same exquisite privilege of standing before God. This is your wisdom and this is your life.

BOB SORGE is "the speaker who can't talk"—that is, he is reduced to a whisper because of a debilitating vocal injury he suffered over twenty years ago. Through the journey, God has given him an empowering message that explores God's purposes in fiery trials. It's not the fire that changes you but your pursuit of God in the fire that changes you. Bob has a unique way of helping us process our journey so we stay in the race and overcome. Whether you're reading one of his books or listening to him, you're about to receive a word from the heart of God that will strengthen your faith and draw you into greater intimacy with Jesus.

LIGHT ONE CANDLE

by Joshua Mills

Jesus again spoke to them, saying, "I am the Light of the world; he who follows Me will not walk in the darkness, but will have the Light of life"
(John 8:12 NASB).

Christmas is a celebration of light, and therefore much of our seasonal imagery and many of our holiday traditions revolve around light. Thousands of years ago, the first Christmas was marked by angels that suddenly appeared to humble shepherds who were keeping watch over their flocks in the fields of Judea. Those angels were surrounded by brilliant light and said that they had come to announce the birth of the Savior, who was given to the earth as the Light of the World, *"the Light of life."* The night those angels appeared, the heavens over Judea were lit up with a myriad of stars, each one giving off a radiant light.

A favorite Christmas hymn describes that night well:

Oh, holy night, the stars are brightly shining

It is the night of our dear Savior's birth.

Long lay the world in sin and error pining

Till He appeared and the soul felt its worth.[1]

In that moment, Jesus' light shined upon us, and everything changed. Light…I love it. Don't you?

It seems that all my favorite Christmas traditions involve the presence of light. For instance, I always like to decorate the outside of my home with Christmas lights, and I love to take my family for drives around the city at Christmastime in search of other homes that are sparkling with untold numbers of twinkling lights. At the height of the Christmas season, homes and businesses everywhere are decorated with beautiful lights. Light… we just can't get enough of it! Can we?

At our home, we decorate our family Christmas tree, set up in the living room, with many lights, but then each individual member of the family has their own Christmas tree in their bedroom, also decorated with lights. Every brilliant light that is lit during Christmas is a representation of Jesus, the Light of Life. We just can't have too much light.

God's Word declares:

The Light shines in the darkness, and the darkness did not comprehend it (John 1:5 NASB).

For God, who said, "Light shall shine out of darkness," is the One who has shone in our hearts to give the Light of the knowledge of the glory of God in the face of Christ (2 Corinthians 4:6 NASB).

On a few occasions, we've had the privilege of visiting the famous Christmas Markets of Germany, and it has always been a very special experience to see the explosion of lights displayed there. Some of those markets date back hundreds of years. From traditional handicrafts and intricate ornaments to tasty local delicacies and sweet-scented wines, there's absolutely nothing you can't find in a German Christmas market, whether you choose to browse the most popular ones or visit those hidden in some quaint medieval village.

In addition to festive shopping, Germany's best Christmas markets offer visitors an enchanting experience that combines culture, entertainment, and holiday cheer in a magical fairytale-like setting. It was at one of these Christmas markets in Frankfurt that we were introduced to and subsequently purchased our first Christmas pyramid. It is a wooden carousel of many levels that each contain a nativity scene, and the whole tower revolves, powered by the flame of four candles that flicker beneath its umbrella fan. Light…it is so powerful!

There is something so miraculous about the flickering glow of candlelight, especially during the Christmas or Advent season. It is light of a very special nature. Light…it changes the atmosphere of our lives! It renews our weary souls!

The word "advent" means the arrival of a notable person, thing, or event, and during the holiday season we have the opportunity to celebrate the arrival of Jesus Christ coming in the flesh as a Child in the manger of Bethlehem. We who call Him Lord have experienced His coming to us personally, as our Savior and Redeemer, as we welcomed Him into our hearts and allowed Him to take full control of our lives. And we also have the hope of Him one day returning in glory to reign as King over all at His Second Coming. Jesus is the Light of our lives, and one day every knee will bow before Him. Light… there is no light like Jesus!

In liturgical traditions, the celebration of Advent is observed over the four weeks leading up to Christmas, each week corresponding with one of four candles representing hope, love, joy, and peace, or sometimes purity. There is often a fifth candle. This is the Christ candle, which is lit on either Christmas Eve or Christmas Day. Light…we all need more of it!

Even my favorite Christmas songs revolve around the theme of light. A few years ago, when I was preparing to record a holiday album entitled "Christmas Miracle," I spent months listening to hundreds of traditional and nontraditional seasonal songs, searching for just the right selections to include. My desire was to record an album that contained more than the standard listening fair, and instead offer something special for the listener, some real light.

In my search, I came across a song called "Light One Candle." It was written by Paul Yarrow and originally recorded by the singing group Peter, Paul, and Mary. "Light One Candle" is an anthem for the Hanukkah season, and although I am not Jewish, I felt strangely connected to the song.

The lyrics of the chorus declare:

Don't let the light go out!

It's lasted for so many years!

Don't let the light go out!

Let it shine through our hope and our tears.

I love that chorus. Don't let the light go out! That is our commission in this world of darkness. Light...the whole world needs it!

In researching the history of Hanukkah, I quickly discovered that it commemorates the restoration of Jewish worship at the holy temple in Jerusalem in the second century BC. A Jewish priest named Judas Maccabeus led a revolt against the oppression of the Seleucid Empire (167-160 BC) and, when victory was achieved, he then worked with his soldiers to cleanse and repair the temple. To his utter dismay, he discovered that the temple had been desecrated with Greek idols and statues of false gods and goddesses and that the many instruments used for proper worship of the one true God had gone missing or been broken, including the golden menorah. They worked tirelessly to repair the temple and return it to holy worship.

When Judas Maccabeus and his men had finished their work of cleansing and repairing the temple, they decided to have a dedication ceremony. As part of this dedication, they would relight the golden menorah. The problem was that, even after scouring the surrounding countryside, they had found only enough oil to last for one day. They decided to light the menorah anyway and, by a miracle of God, the oil they had secured burned for eight straight days.

God had seen their hearts and sustained their provision in a supernatural way. It was a moment of great rejoicing. This is how Hanukkah or *Chanukah*—meaning "dedication," now an eight-day celebration—became known as the Festival of Lights. It is a celebration of renewed hope. The light that shone in that temple in the second century BC was miraculous and brought glory to the one true and living God, and He is still the Father of Lights today.

> *Every good thing given and every perfect gift is from above, coming down from the Father of lights, with whom there is no variation or shifting shadow* (James 1:17 NASB).

During Advent this year, we should remember that Jesus is the true Light of the world and also that our

God is the God of miracles. We have been given the Holy Spirit flame, and, along with that flame, we have been given the responsibility of spreading His light everywhere we go. We cannot afford to hide our light. We must share it, lighting a candle wherever we can. Light… it quickly dispels darkness!

The price has been paid for our salvation by Jesus Himself, the Light of the World, but many sacrifices have also been made by servants of Christ, many of them martyrs who faithfully carried the Spirit-filled Gospel to the ends of the earth. They were amazing lights in their time and place. What can you and I do today in the twenty-first century to spread God's light? Light…that is our calling!

You may not be a preacher of the Gospel, and you may not be called upon to give your life in physical sacrifice, but you *can* spread God's light in many other ways. The first and most important way you can spread light to the dark world around you is to live out the Gospel before others. Do your spouse and children recognize the light of Christ in you in the home? Do your coworkers see you as light in the workplace? Are you a light to your community? Are you loving and kind, joyful, and hopeful? In other words, are you a light in the darkness? Light…that is our destiny!

Even if you are not a preacher of the Gospel, each of us can speak about what blesses us, what we're happy about, what we love. During the Christmas season, people seem to be much more open to the supernatural realms of God than at any other time of the year. People sing songs about "Christ the Lord," they adorn their homes with decorations of angels and stars, and their hearts seem conditioned to be generous givers more than at any other time of year.

Yes, many have sought to materialize this season, but you and I must focus, instead, on the opportunities God places before us to release the light of His glory during this wonderful time of the year and, in this way, spread light in the surrounding darkness:

> For you were formerly darkness, but now you are **Light in the Lord; walk as children of Light** (for the fruit of the Light consists in all goodness and righteousness and truth), trying to learn what is pleasing to the Lord (Ephesians 5:8-10 NASB).

> But you are a chosen race, a royal priesthood, a holy nation, a people for God's own possession, so that you may **proclaim the excellencies of Him who has called you out of darkness into His marvelous light** (1 Peter 2:9 NASB).

Light…it sets us free and makes us shine!

Will you choose to be God's light this Christmas season? If that is your desire, start by lighting one candle. When you do that, you are releasing light that will pierce the darkest places during the darkest times.

Prayer

Now, please pray with me:

Father of Lights, thank You for being the Light of my life. Every day I now walk in the light of Your love. Every day I now bask in the glow of Your glory presence. I cannot praise You enough. You literally light up my life. I ask You to make me the light You want me to be in the darkness that surrounds me. Rather than curse the darkness, I choose to light a candle and thereby show others the way to Your love and light. Thank You for this privilege and help me to be worthy of it. Help me to be light in my world. In Jesus' name, amen!

JOSHUA MILLS is an internationally recognized ordained minister of the Gospel, as well as a recording artist, keynote conference speaker, and author of more than twenty books and spiritual training manuals.

He is well known for his unique insights into the glory realm, prophetic sound, and the supernatural atmosphere that he carries. Wherever Joshua ministers, the Word of God is confirmed by miraculous signs and wonders that testify of Jesus Christ. For more than twenty years, he has helped people discover the life-shifting truth of salvation, healing, and deliverance for spirit, soul and body.

Joshua and his wife, Janet, co-founded International Glory Ministries, and have ministered on six continents in over seventy-five nations around the world. Featured in several film documentaries and print articles, including Charisma and Worship Leader Magazine, together, they have ministered to millions around the world through radio, television, and online webcasts, including appearances on TBN, Daystar, GodTV, *It's Supernatural!* with Sid Roth, *100 Huntley Street,* and *Everlasting Love* with Patricia King.

Their ministry is located in both Palm Springs, California, and London, Ontario, Canada, where they live with their three children: Lincoln, Liberty, and Legacy.

Visit their website: www.joshuamills.com.

ENDNOTE

1. Music composed by Adolphe Adam in 1847 to the French poem "Minuit, chrétiens" by Placide Cappeau (1808-1877).

BLESSED ARE THOSE WHO ARE NOT OFFENDED BY HIS COMING

by Larry Sparks

The Savior—yes, the Messiah, the Lord—has been born today in Bethlehem, the city of David!
(Luke 2:11 NLT)

urely, the angels' announcement perplexed the shepherds. The Savior, the Messiah, *the Lord*, had come! Good news, for sure. I am certain these lowly Jewish shepherds had some concept of what the angelic host were proclaiming. I often wonder if they started to collectively imagine what this scene would look like. What would the birth of the Lord look like? *Born in a palace, surrounded by nobility,* perhaps? *Born among the Pharisees and religious teachers of the day, welcomed as the long-awaited and prophesied Messiah,* maybe?

I have to wonder if the following statement by the angels confused, perplexed, or even offended the shepherds—at least, offended their minds: *"And you will recognize him by this sign: You will find a baby wrapped snugly in strips of cloth, lying in a manger"* (Luke 2:12 NLT). *Wait, did we hear that right? You said that the Lord would be wrapped snugly in…strips of cloth, lying in a…manger?*

Offense is not always an expression of anger or bitterness; sometimes, we experience offense when everything we thought to be the way it is, is confronted and challenged. How could it be that the King of kings would be born in a manger, surrounded by the animals that these shepherds were very familiar with leading, cleaning up after, and taking care of? Let's ponder this a little further before we return to how the shepherds ultimately responded. After all, the angels essentially announced to them that the greatest move of God to ever hit the planet had touched down in Bethlehem and that they were being invited to participate!

CHRISTMAS IS JUST OFFENSIVE!

The surroundings of Jesus' birth were not as Christmas-card appropriate as we often think. To even entertain the prospect of the Messiah being laid in an animal feeding trough would be undoubtedly offensive to many of the religiously minded elites of the day. And yet, that is why we celebrate all these years later. We celebrate the offensive unfolding of Christmas, which points to the God who moves according to His desires, the Lord who is not beyond condescending Himself, and the King who goes low because He is searching for those who are, likewise, humble of heart to greet and receive His move.

God will bypass kings and rulers to be met by shepherds. It's not that He is against those of status or nobility; far from it. The wise men (magi) reoriented their lives to seek after Him. But their quest was motivated by the very characteristics that position us to experience a move of God, both at the birth of Jesus and in our contemporary world—humility and hunger.

Perhaps, though, the story of Christmas is more relevant than we think. For two thousand years since the death and resurrection of Jesus, history has been marked by revivals and spiritual awakenings. We often call these "moves of God." Dr. Michael Brown has said, "You can have controversy without revival, but you cannot have revival without controversy." Something confronts our pride and arrogance when God moves, for His movement is always out of the box and unconventional. It's not anti-biblical, as some suggest; it's not "strange fire," distracting people from the core message of the Gospel. But rest assured, when God moves, there are always those who reject His movement because it does not compute with how *they think* He should move. And yet, there are always shepherds and wise men, Annas and Simeons to welcome His move *when He does come*. And thus, we return to the Christmas story.

The King of kings born in a manger didn't make sense to many. Crowds did not surround Mary and Joseph as this move of God was birthed into the earth. But for those who received and welcomed Him, they were able to participate in the greatest move of God that would ever grace the planet—Heaven coming to Earth in the form of Mary's precious baby boy.

Blessed Is...

"Blessed is the one who is not offended by me" (Matthew 11:6). This seems like a strange observation to make concerning the Christmas story, especially using a passage of Scripture where Jesus was responding to the disciples of John the Baptist. The reality is, John sent messengers to Jesus basically asking, "Are *you* really the Messiah or should we wait for someone else—someone who will function and act more like we expected?"

Most likely John asked this because he was in prison and it didn't seem like his vindication or deliverance was coming. The Savior-Messiah was not functioning as the Conquering Warrior whom many had anticipated. If He was, then the powers that imprisoned John the Baptist would be overthrown and a new heavenly golden age would be established right there, on the spot. But this was not happening. Everything that was unfolding just didn't make sense. And this is where we pick up the Christmas story—something that, at face value, didn't make much sense either. It's right there, in the middle of a story that makes little sense, that we are introduced to how God moves.

Two thousand years later, we celebrate the Christmas story with great fanfare and joy. However, as the narrative was unfolding in its time, Mary and Joseph were not experiencing conditions that necessarily merited celebration. Much of it, quite frankly, seemed offensive. Not the pristine environment for the King of kings to be birthed into. It simply did not make sense that God Almighty would be birthed in a humble manger, wrapped in swaddling clothes, surrounded by barnyard animals. And yet, Heaven deliberately set everything up, even prophesying the details hundreds of years in advance.

No Room for the Move of God

This may sound like a strange invitation for a devotional reading, but I encourage you to let the Christmas story offend you. Reconsider the details surrounding the Messiah's birth and really process as to whether that makes sense.

Take this one Scripture, for example, and consider how utterly outlandish the circumstances are:

And she gave birth to her firstborn son and wrapped him in swaddling cloths and laid him in a manger, because there was no place for them in the inn (Luke 2:7).

No Place at the Inn

First, Mary and Joseph were rejected by the inn and thus, the pregnant mother was not able to give birth to Jesus in hospitable conditions. Why? *There was no place for them—no room for the move of God.* This observation made by Luke carries implications into our modern world today. It would make sense for Jesus to be born at least in the comfort of an inn, the ancient equivalent to a hotel or at minimum, bed and breakfast. After all, if He wasn't going to be granted a regal birth in a palace or Priestly place among the religious elite, at least give Him the decency of sanitary, clean conditions. No. I believe the inn's rejection is meant to offend us. The fact that Jesus was not born in a palace and that Joseph and Mary were turned away from the inn tells us that we will often find Jesus moving, and birthing new things, in environments that don't make sense because places that should have welcomed Him actually rejected Him. The people who should have received His love and grace denied Him. The places that should have celebrated the move of His Spirit and power said, "No, we don't want *that*." Let's not be the inn that rejects Him—let's be a manger that receives Him.

Laid in a Manger

Second, Jesus was not surrounded by a royal or priestly entourage at His birth. He was laid in a manger. Since there was no room at the inn, a place that would have made sense for His birth, they had to find alternative accommodations quickly. The Christ-child was coming, ready or not! If not in a palace or inn, then in a lowly, humble manger. This reminds us that moves of God are always birthed in humble places. God is attracted to humility and lowliness, as Peter writes: *"God resists you when you are proud but multiplies grace and favor when you are humble"* (1 Peter 5:5 TPT).

The great Advents of God—beginning with the humble Incarnation that Christmas celebrates, continuing with the great awakenings throughout church history, and culminating with His glorious appearing at the end of the age—require a humility of heart to see and receive what God is doing.

May our hearts be like the manger that warmly received the Savior of the world upon His first advent. It didn't make sense. If we allowed it, all of the details of the Incarnation would offend our minds because His movement was so contrary to how many thought He *should* come. And although the crowd was sparse at the manger, there was a remnant eager and ready to receive the Messiah. May we be eager and ready, likewise, to receive Jesus today as He moves on earth through the wind of His Spirit.

RUN TO WHERE GOD IS MOVING...EVEN IF IT DOESN'T MAKE SENSE!

So, how do we respond to God moving today? In our lives? Families? Cities and regions? In our spheres of influence, jobs, and professions? In our churches? The fact is, God *is* moving, and He is seeking people who see what He is doing and will partner with His movement.

Go back and consider the shepherd's elaborate blueprint for accommodating a move of God. That's a joke, as such was far from the truth. It didn't take a theologian or rabbi to tell the shepherds how to respond.

Angels announced the birth of the Messiah. Then they described the lowly, humble, offensive conditions of His birth. I'm sure the shepherds were faced with a choice at this point. *Could this really be the One who would deliver us and liberate us from oppression? Could this be the long-awaited and prophesied Messiah? I mean, how is this even possible considering the conditions He is being born into? Swaddling clothes, lying in a manger? That doesn't sound like God to me.* Their minds, I'm sure, were racing and exploring all of the options. What did they do?

> When the angels had gone away from them into heaven, the shepherds began saying one to another, "Let us go straight to Bethlehem, and see this [wonderful] thing that has happened which the Lord has made known to us." So they went in a hurry and found their way

to Mary and Joseph, and the Baby as He lay in the manger (Luke 2:15-16 Amplified Bible).

So, what provoked the shepherds' historic response causing them to be part of that intimate group who welcomed the Messiah to the earth? They went low. They surrendered their expectations of how God should move and instead embraced a lowly King who would be found by the humble seeker. They surrendered their need for God to fit into their framework and chose to embrace Him on *His terms.* This is the key to participating in any move of God, from the great revivals of history, to the activity of God in your everyday life— instead of trying to get God to move like *we* want Him to, we intently look for how He is moving. And we evaluate, "Does this look like God? Does this sound like God? Does this represent God's nature and character as revealed in the Scriptures?" It doesn't matter what we think God should do, or how we think He should respond. God is not subject to our thought processes; He will always act and move in harmony with His eternal, unchanging Word.

Author and prayer leader Dutch Sheets, put it this way: "As with the wise men who followed a star and found a stable, Mary who rocked a son and raised a Savior, and the disciples who longed for a crown and looked at a cross, He continues to surprise us." May we ever be open and receptive to the surprises of a moving God!

PRAYER

Lord, help me not to be offended by how You move. So, I ask You, right now, to remind me of Christmas. Remind me of the shepherds who ran to embrace what You were doing, even if it sounded ridiculous. Help me to run like they did toward You. Help me to always be looking for Your countenance. Fashion my heart to be a manger, a place that receives the move and manifestation of Your Spirit, even if it comes packaged or presented in a way I didn't expect. You know my heart, Lord. I don't want anything fake or false. I don't want anything that's not of You. But at the same time, I don't want to assume too much. I don't want to reject Your movement, Your activity, and Your purposes because they don't fit in my paradigm. Open my eyes, humble my heart, and help me to hurry toward Your movement in my life!

NO MORE GLOOM

by Brian Simmons

Heaven couldn't contain itself! The thin line between Heaven and earth peeled back. Countless numbers of angels cascaded onto the hillside near Bethlehem ready to burst forth with high praises. With a light the earth had never seen before, myriads of angels appeared glowing with Heaven's glory before the startled shepherds. First, the glory of God manifested, shining all around them, then the trumpet voice of the mighty angel proclaimed the Good News to the whole world. Rank upon rank of angels spiraled into formation in the blinding glory. Unable to hold it back they let it roar:

Glory to God in the highest heaven, and on earth peace to those on whom his favor rests (Luke 2:14 New International Version).

Imagine that sight! All because a Child is born. The appearing of Jesus in human history means the end of gloom, despair, and hopelessness. The scourge of sin and death is lifted off the lives of those who believe in Jesus Christ. Sadly, there is gloom everywhere in this fallen world. Suicide and self-destructive tendencies are on the rise. Depression and all that brings with it is like a cloud of gloom over too many. Our lives are precious before God. How do I know? Because God sent His Son to receive gloom and replace it with glory!

I will never forget the birth of each of our three children. A child is born to the Simmons' house! A few years later…another, and then another. To us daughters were born! A son was given to us. None of them were planned by Mom and Dad, but all three were planned from before time was born. This triple gift given to us came in the form of two darling girls and a son of delight. Yes, a child can change the world. They sure changed ours!

Praise must rise from our hearts this Christmas season. What we have before us is not the end of the world, but the end of gloom. This truth must grip our hearts as we look at our lives today. Ponder the words of Isaiah, the seer-prophet, written over 2,700 years ago:

*Nevertheless, there will be **no more gloom** for those who were in distress. In the past he humbled the land of*

Zebulun and the land of Naphtali, but in the future
he will honor…. The people walking in darkness have
seen a great light; on those living in the land of deep
darkness a light has dawned. You have enlarged the
nation and increased their joy; they rejoice before you
as people rejoice at the harvest, as warriors rejoice when
dividing the plunder. For as in the day of Midian's
defeat, you have shattered the yoke that burdens them,
the bar across their shoulders, the rod of their oppressor
(Isaiah 9:1-4 New International Version).

Do you feel the ecstatic joy of this passage? God, through the miraculous birth of His Son, has lifted gloom, despair, and oppression off the hearts of His people! Radiant light now bursts into those dark places, where shame has made a home. The birth of Christ is a prophecy that every dark shadow in your life will be removed! All that once brought us shame is taken away by the work of God's Son on the Cross. Now, only joy remains. We are soon to be those who are overwhelmed with joy because of the great harvest that is coming. We will gleefully enjoy the spoils of the victories of Jesus. Chains broken, emotional despair and grief lifted. That is what Christmas means to me.

In the place where devastation has robbed hope, He will appear! The land of Zebulun and Naphtali along with all of Israel was punished by God for their disobedience. They had turned a deaf ear to the prophet Amos and the appeals of Hosea and Isaiah the prophet. They predicted an invasion that would come if the people did not repent, and the people didn't. Yet even during such warning and impending judgment there was a Promise—a Light that would come and release healing rays. No matter what happens, this Light will be present and shining on tender hearts until the whole earth is bathed in this Light (Isaiah 60:1).

Zebulun and the land of Naphtali were the very first territories the attacking armies of Assyria conquered, plunging the nation into gloom and darkness. Zebulun and Naphtali became symbols of those who couldn't endure, fallen ones who could not resist. Yet they will be the ones honored and esteemed on the day the Light shines. That's always how God acts! He chooses the places in our lives where we have the most disgrace and shame, and there brings His light. Our past failures become prophecies of a future victory! *No failure is final when Jesus is here.*

So why would Isaiah point us to the birth of this Baby and tell us that gloom is gone forever the day this child was born? Because the Light has come. When Light shines, darkness must run and hide. Jesus Christ, even as an infant, was and is the brightest Light to ever come to this sin-darkened planet. How many lives have been transformed by His Light? How many hearts have been healed when rays of His Light shined upon them?

The day of no more gloom is the day you allow Jesus into your life and let Him reign as King. Each time more of Christ is birthed in us, there is light. Gloom disappears, grace takes its place. The ending of night is the shining of His Light. Just as darkness and night have boundaries—they have an end (Genesis 1:4)—so the Lord will cause your gloom to end, the shadows to flee.

He is the One who says, "It will last this long and not a day longer!" God begins in darkness and brings to the day. The evening and the morning were the first day. Are you in the dark? Your night will turn to day. Be faithful always. Pray your way into His Light.

More than once I was convinced that my darkness would not end. Have you ever faced depression and gloom? I have. Sometimes it seems like demons and people and circumstances all line up against me and point out my failures, and they are miserable ones. My sins become amplified and God's voice muted. My own heart had me convinced that my twilight steps would drag me deeper into darkness. Then He stepped in! My Great Light became my Salvation. The only time gloom is ended in my life is when I crave the Light and allow Him to penetrate my fears and distress. What Jesus has done for Zebulun, He will do for me. What this Bright Light has done for Naphtali, He will surely do for you!

The people who walked in darkness have seen a great light" (Isaiah 9:2). This Scripture is fulfilled every time you feel the darkness closing in. There's a new day dawning each time our hearts turn to the Light. *"Even if darkness overtakes them, sunrise-brilliance will come bursting through…"* (Psalm 112:4 TPT). This great Light coming to light our way is Jesus Christ. As Jesus appeared as a baby, the shining star highlighted His birthplace. Through the preaching of the True Prophet, the star turned into the rays of a sunrise. He had come to bring healing in His ways.

All the people of the earth walk in spiritual darkness, not knowing where they are going. Jesus is the Radiant Light who has come to take us home. It is God who opens our eyes to that Light. He opens our blinded eyes and we fall in love with Him. This Radiant Light includes His teachings, His miracles, His pure life lived before the Father. It is the Light of joy, the Light of revelation, the Light of deliverance. Jesus Christ is the Light of direction for the lost and comfort for the hurting. Jesus' birth signals an end of night and the beginning of morning.

They once lived in the shadows of death, but now a glorious light has dawned! Our lives are lived continually in the shadow of death—like a giant grim reaper who stands over us all, casting his dark shadow over our ways. We are all in danger when we live in the shadow of death. Death touches us all. We lose loved ones. Relationships die. Dreams die. Hopes are crushed. *"Mortals, born of woman, are of few days and full of trouble"* (Job 14:1 New International Version).

But we are not born of woman, we are born of the Spirit and made new creations. Our days may be spent in the Light of His countenance, basking in His glory. The sweet, dawning Light of Jesus has taken away the shadows—fears and doubts. The battle of the ages is over. Light has conquered darkness. We must choose to dwell in the Light and allow its increase to be imparted within us.

When Christ comes into us, He brings Kingdom authority to subdue, conquer, and overthrow all that hinders the full release of His glory within us. Emmanuel is now with you to dispense His life and restore every fallen aspect of your life.

JOY TO THE WORLD!

A feast of joy is waiting for you. Fast from your pain, problems, and disappointments and rejoice in the good things God is unveiling in these last days. Revival joy is about to break forth! So full and so glorious it defies description.

> *You love him passionately although you did not see him, but through believing in him you are saturated with an ecstatic joy, indescribably sublime and* **immersed** *in glory* (1 Peter 1:8 TPT).

This joy is not exclusive to humanity—the angels get to partake of this Christmas joy! For the first time in all eternity, the angels saw God's face, it was the face of a baby. Bethlehem's manger was like a throne for angels to come and worship, no wonder they sang and rejoiced, for God had entered His creation, for God took upon Himself the likeness of humanity.

> *For the mystery of righteousness is truly amazing! He was revealed as a human being, and as our great High*

Priest in the Spirit! Angels gazed upon him as a man…!
Yes, great is this mystery of righteousness! (1 Timothy
3:16 TPT).

The mystery of the incarnation of Christ must grip
us this season with great joy! Angels saw in the form of
a baby the One they had worshipped and served from
the beginning. They stand in awe and worship night and
day before this One, unable to see a form or a face—but
on that morning, they saw the face of a newborn. They
gazed upon the face and rejoiced with joy.

Our joy is the joy of the Feast of Tabernacles. The
two great joys of the human heart come at a time of harvest and a time of victory. Human celebration at these
two times knows no bounds. As the increase is brought
in, victory is experienced. What greater joy is there in
Heaven and earth than when souls are saved? The plunder of souls is divided, and all are blessed: *"Even the lame
will take their share"* (Isaiah 33:23 NLT).

Reflection

A sign of the moving of God among us to fulfill this
promise is an outbreaking of joy! He fills our mouths
with laughter as a sign that the great ingathering of
harvest is here (Psalm 126). The Gospel will always
bring joy, and those who receive good news will rejoice
(Psalm 67:4).

Joy to the World!

No more let sins and sorrows grow

Nor thorns infest the ground

He comes to make His blessings flow

Far as the curse is found, far as the curse is found

Far as, far as the curse is found.

DR. BRIAN SIMMONS is known as a passionate lover of God. After a dramatic conversion to Christ, Brian knew that God was calling him to go to the unreached people of the world and present the Gospel of God's grace to all who would listen. With his wife Candice and their three children, they spent eight years in the tropical rain forest of the Darien Province of Panama as a church planter, translator, and consultant. Brian was involved in the Paya-Kuna New Testament translation project. He studied linguistics and Bible translation principles with New Tribes Mission. After their ministry in the jungle, Brian was instrumental in planting a thriving church in New England (U.S.), and now travels full time as a speaker and Bible teacher. He is currently the lead translator for The Passion Translation Project which will produce a new, dynamic version of the Bible that promises to shape the spirituality of coming generations. He has been happily married to Candice for forty-six years and is known to boast regularly of his three children and six grandchildren.

22

REMEMBER
THE DRAGON

by John Eldredge

Herod was furious when he learned that the wise men had outwitted him. He sent soldiers to kill all the boys in and around Bethlehem who were two years old and under, based on the wise men's report of the star's first appearance. Herod's brutal action fulfilled what God had spoken through the prophet Jeremiah: "A cry was heard in Ramah—weeping and great mourning. Rachel weeps for her children, refusing to be comforted, for they are dead" (Matthew 2:16-18 NLT).

I have never seen this part of the story portrayed in any pageant or manger scene. For those of us raised in middle America, this genocide was completely left out of our Christmas understanding. Our visions of the nativity were shaped by classic Christmas cards and by the lovely crèche displays in parks, on church lawns, and on many coffee tables. And while I still love those tableaus very much, I am convinced they are an almost total rewrite of the story.

On the night before the military "massacre of the innocents," as it has come to be called, another urgent moment took place:

> After the wise men were gone, an angel of the Lord appeared to Joseph in a dream. "Get up! Flee to Egypt with the child and his mother," the angel said. "Stay there until I tell you to return, because Herod is going to try to kill him." That night Joseph left for Egypt with the child and Mary, his mother, and they stayed there until Herod's death... (Matthew 2:13-15 NLT).

This, too, seems right out of the devastation in the Middle East—refugees fleeing for their lives, taking cover in a foreign country. But I haven't seen this portrayed in the lovely imagery surrounding Christmastime either. I understand, the imagery is dear to many of us, but it is also profoundly *deceiving;* it creates all sorts of warm feelings, associations, and expectations—many quite subconscious—of what the nature of the Christian life is going to be like for us.

The omissions are, in fact, dangerous. The equivalent of ignoring the movements of Isis.

Contrast your associations with Christmas night to this description given to us from Heaven's point of view:

I saw a woman…She was pregnant, and she cried out in the pain of labor as she awaited her delivery. Suddenly, I witnessed in heaven another significant event. I saw a large red dragon with seven heads and ten horns, with seven crowns on his heads. His tail dragged down one-third of the stars, which he threw to the earth. He stood before the woman as she was about to give birth to her child, ready to devour the baby as soon as it was born. She gave birth to a boy who was to rule all nations with an iron rod…

Then there was war in heaven. Michael and the angels under his command fought the dragon and his angels. And the dragon lost the battle and was forced out of Heaven. This great dragon—the ancient serpent called the devil, or satan, the one deceiving the whole world—was thrown down to the earth with all his angels… And when the dragon realized that he had been thrown down to the earth, he pursued the woman who had given birth to the child. But she was given two wings like those of a great eagle. This allowed her to fly to a place prepared for her in the wilderness, where she would be cared for and protected from the dragon for a time, times, and half a time…Then the dragon… declared war against the rest of her children—all who keep God's commandments and confess that they belong to Jesus (see Revelation 12).

Startling. Vivid. Disturbing for sure. And an essential part of the story.

I would pay good money to have a nativity scene with this included. Not only would it capture our imagination, I think, but it would also better prepare us to celebrate the holidays and to go on to live the story Christmas invites us into.

Yes—Christmas is the glow of candlelight on golden straw, and a baby sleeping in a manger. It is starlight, shepherds in a field, and the visit of the magi from the East. *But Christmas is also an invasion.* The Kingdom of God striking at the heart of the kingdom of darkness with violent repercussions.

I think if this had informed our understanding of the birth of Christ, it would have better prepared us for our own lives, and the events unfolding in the world today. I think far fewer of us would be so…*puzzled* by the way things are going. For as J.R.R. Tolkien warned, "It does not do to leave a live dragon out of your calculations, if you live near him."

Prayer

Heavenly Father, may we never forget "the rest of the story" of Christmas and the turbulent times when Jesus was born—and that we have inherited through the evil that permeates the world. May we also never forget, dear Lord, the love and compassion You showered upon this world in the form of an innocent babe—who lived and died to wash away our sin, leaving us clean and redeemed.

JOHN ELDREDGE is a best-selling author, counselor, and a teacher. He is the president of Ransomed Heart, a ministry devoted to helping people discover the heart of God, recover their own hearts in God's love, and learn to live in God's kingdom. John and his wife Stasi live near Colorado Springs, Colorado.

ONLY BELIEVE

by Katherine Ruonala

The Christmas season is a wonderful opportunity to remember the goodness, faithfulness, and supernatural power of God to fulfill His promises to us. Picture this, a young virgin is shocked and surprised by a face-to-face encounter with an angel announcing she was going to supernaturally conceive and give birth to the Son of God. The message from God was that He was going to do something impossible in Mary's life.

Now in the sixth month the angel Gabriel was sent by God to a city of Galilee named Nazareth, to a virgin betrothed to a man whose name was Joseph, of the house of David. The virgin's name was Mary. And having come in, the angel said to her, "Rejoice, highly favored one, the Lord is with you; blessed are you among women!"

But when she saw him, she was troubled at his saying, and considered what manner of greeting this was. Then the angel said to her, "Do not be afraid, Mary, for you have found favor with God. And behold, you will conceive in your womb and bring forth a Son, and shall call His name Jesus. He will be great, and will be called the Son of the Highest; and the Lord God will give Him the throne of His father David. And He will reign over the house of Jacob forever, and of His kingdom there will be no end."

Then Mary said to the angel, "How can this be, since I do not know a man?"

And the angel answered and said to her, "The Holy Spirit will come upon you, and the power of the Highest will overshadow you; therefore, also, that Holy One who is to be born will be called the Son of God. Now indeed, Elizabeth your relative has also conceived a son in her old age; and this is now the sixth month for her who was called barren. For with God nothing will be impossible" (Luke 1:26-37 NKJV).

Like this promise to Mary, prophetic words and biblical promises can often seem outrageous and astonishing. Some people react with a wait-and-see attitude, believing that if the promise is for them it will just happen and that no faith or response is needed. But it is important to remember that prophetic words are generally not inevitabilities but invitations waiting for our response. I love Mary's response to God's promise,

> *Behold the maidservant of the Lord! Let it be to me according to your word* (Luke 1:38 NJKV).

Mary made a decision to believe God and receive the word. And the word was implanted in her, and grew within until she gave birth to the promise. And the word became flesh and was manifested.

GOD'S PROMISES

Like Mary, we also need to respond to the promises of God for our lives. Sometimes though, we can have trouble believing that we are worthy of receiving His promises. The Bible tells us that through Christ we have become coheirs with Him, which means we have access to every promise in the Bible, no matter what race, gender, or background we come from. F.F. Bosworth used to say that "Faith begins where the will of God is known." Knowing that the gift of salvation has qualified us to be coheirs of all the promises empowers us to believe and receive them. The message of Christmas is that through the gift of Jesus, believers have been qualified to inherit His promises.

So now we can respond like Mary to God's promises, *"Be it unto me according to your word."*

The Bible tells us that all of God's promises are yes and amen to us (2 Corinthians 1:20).

They are laid out for us like food on a banqueting table waiting for us to get up and eat. First Timothy 1:18 tells us how to respond to this bountiful feast by encouraging us to wage warfare with the prophetic promises made over us. The weapons we wage war with are also explained to us in Scripture. For example, Proverbs 18:21 tells us that our tongues are deadly weapons that have the power to bring life or death. So we can wage war with our words by declaring in faith what God has promised.

God has given us so many prophetic invitations. For example, He promises that the same works He did, greater works will we do. That seems impossible, but like Gabriel told Mary, with God, nothing is impossible. I have seen God open blind eyes and deaf ears. I have seen Him make the crippled walk and heal those who had been given no medical hope in the natural.

I can testify to the reality of God's delight in fulfilling His promises to us. He is the same yesterday, today, and forever! If you need healing in your body, start today by declaring that by His stripes you are healed. See your sickness on His body and declare that He has borne your sorrow. Many are the afflictions of the righteous, but the Lord delivers us from them all! (See Psalm 34:19.)

I love Elizabeth's response to Mary when she saw the pregnant teenager:

Blessed is she who believed, for there will be a fulfillment of those things which were told her from the Lord (Luke 1:45 NKJV).

INVITATION

Because Mary believed, she was able to receive. God's heart for each of us is to believe that the gift of His Son qualifies us to be heirs of all His promises. By faith you can step into the prophetic destiny God has for you by believing God and lining up your words with His. Nothing is impossible with God. Only believe!

KATHERINE RUONALA has a prophetic and healing ministry and travels internationally as a conference speaker bringing a message of love and hope to the nations. Katherine carries a strong prophetic and miracle anointing with many being instantly healed in her meetings. Reaching across denominational walls, her ministry is also used to spread the fires of revival and ignite a fresh passion in the hearts of believers to go deeper in their relationship with God.

Katherine hosts her own television show *Katherine Ruonala TV* and is author of the best-selling books *Living in the Miraculous: How God's Love is Expressed Through the Supernatural, Wilderness to Wonders: Embracing the Power of*

Process and *Life With The Holy Spirit: Enjoying Intimacy With The Spirit of God.*

Katherine's husband Tom Ruonala is an accomplished businessman and serves as the Honorary Consul of Finland in Brisbane. Katherine is the founder and coordinator of the Australian Prophetic Council and has appeared several times on Sid Roth's *It's Supernatural* television program, CBN and other premium TV shows across the world. Katherine is also bible school graduate and is also a qualified music and singing teacher.

Katherine and Tom have been married for over twenty-eight years and have three beautiful children, Jessica, Emily and Joseph.

INCREASING HIS GOVERNMENTAL RULE FROM THE COURTS OF HEAVEN

by Robert Henderson

I have always loved Christmas. From childhood I have enjoyed everything about this special holiday. I like not only the spiritual substance that this time of year embraces, but even the secular side of it. I know that may get me in trouble, but it's really who I am. I have great and fond memories of things associated with Christmas. I remember the ornaments I made in elementary school that my mother hung on the tree. I remember the fireworks I ignited as a child with my twin brother and nephews.

I remember the presents under the tree on Christmas morning when "Santa Claus" had come. And *no* it didn't warp my belief in Jesus at all as I got older and discovered "Santa" was my parents. I realize there are those who would criticize me and warn that Christmas has pagan roots. They would let me know that as a committed believer I shouldn't so wholeheartedly embrace this season. I just can't help it. I love the atmosphere, the family time, and all the activities that our society and culture embraces. Let me say again, "I love Christmas!"

Having said all this, the most special thing for me about Christmas is the realization that it is the celebration of Jesus' birth. It doesn't matter to me whether December 25 is His actual birthday. I know that it probably isn't. I recognize, however, that Jesus' birth changed everything. Jesus' birth introduced into the earth an expression of the Kingdom of God yet unseen until that time.

Isaiah 9:6-7 prophetically proclaims the effects of Jesus coming into His earth that He created:

> *For unto us a Child is born, unto us a Son is given; and the government will be upon His shoulder. And His name will be called Wonderful, Counselor, Mighty God, Everlasting Father, Prince of Peace.* ***Of the increase of His government and peace there will be no end****, upon the throne of David and over His kingdom,* ***to order it***

and establish it with judgment and justice from that time forward, even forever. The zeal of the Lord of hosts will perform this (NKJV).

Notice that *"Of the increase of His government and peace, there will be no end."* It continues to declare, *"to order it and establish it with judgment and justice."* This is clearly a reference to the judicial activity that would come as a result of Jesus' manifestation as the Son of God. Judgment and justice come from court proceedings. The ever-expanding Kingdom of God will occur because of the judgment and justice being rendered as a result of Jesus being born.

For God's government and peace to come to the earth, evil and wickedness must be dealt with. We will only have *peace on earth* to the degree that God's government is functionally in place. This is what happens from the Courts of Heaven. Everything that would hinder and oppose the purpose of God is dealt with in these Courts. We are part of coming before these Courts and seeing the judgment and justice of God put in place. When we do, the rights of wickedness within our cultures are revoked.

Hebrews 10:12-13 (NKJV) tells us that Jesus is *waiting* for His enemies to be under His footstool. In other words, He is expectantly yearning for all that is contrary to His Kingdom to be subdued before Him:

*But **this Man**, after He had offered one sacrifice for sins forever, sat down at the right hand of God, from that time **waiting till His enemies are made His footstool**.*

What, or rather who, is Jesus waiting on to subdue His enemies? He is waiting on *us* as His people and His church to accomplish this. We are His delegated people granted authority and rights to accomplish these things. This will be done when we take the judgments and justice of His sacrifice, and from the Courts of Heaven execute them into place. Evil will lose its rights to operate and the government, the Kingdom of God with its peace will prevail.

So how should we do this? What are some principles to seeing His enemies become His footstool and His rule over them? First of all, we should realize that when Jesus came, He introduced the Kingdom of God, the government of God, or the rule of God into the earth. Mark 1:14-15 (NKJV) shows us that Jesus' message was declaring the arrival of the Kingdom of God:

> Now after John was put in prison, Jesus came to Galilee, preaching the gospel of the kingdom of God, and saying, "The time is fulfilled, and the kingdom of God is at hand. Repent, and believe in the gospel."

Jesus' arrival on the planet as the Son of God signaled the coming of the government of God on the earth. This is what Daniel saw when he was telling Nebuchadnezzar his dream and giving him the interpretation of it. The last part of the dream saw a stone cut out of a mountain and falling on the feet of all present and coming kingdoms of the earth. This stone then expanded until it filled the whole earth. Daniel 2:44-45 proclaims that this stone is the Kingdom of God that will rule over all other nations:

> And in the days of these kings the God of heaven will set up a kingdom which shall never be destroyed; and the kingdom shall not be left to other people; it shall break in pieces and consume all these kingdoms, and it shall stand forever. Inasmuch as you saw that the stone was cut out of the mountain without hands, and that it broke in pieces the iron, the bronze, the clay, the silver, and the gold—the great God has made known to the king what will come to pass after this. The dream is certain, and its interpretation is sure (NKJV).

Jesus' birth, ministry, sacrifice, resurrection, and ascension back to Heaven set in motion this Kingdom. From the days of Jesus in His earthly manifestation until now, this stone-kingdom government has been expanding. We are part of this process. Any legal rights the devil would still be claiming, we are to stand before the Courts of Heaven and have them revoked. This will facilitate the expansion and increase of the government and peace of the Lord across the nations.

A second important thing we must realize is that *we* are necessary to this process. If we do not take our place before the Courts of Heaven to see satan's rights revoked, what Jesus did will not have the effects God intended. This is why Jesus is *waiting for His enemies to be His footstool.* Isaiah 43:26-28 (NKJV) shows that we must stand and bring God into remembrance as we petition the Courts of Heaven that nations be freed from evil influence:

Put Me in remembrance; let us contend together; **state your case,** *that you may be acquitted. Your first father sinned, and your mediators have transgressed against Me. Therefore I will profane the princes of the sanctuary; I will give Jacob to the curse, and Israel to reproaches.*

We are to *state our case.* If we do not stand in God's judicial place of the Spirit and state our case, nations fall under curses and reproaches. In other words, they live under the influence of the satanic rather than God. We must with boldness and confidence in the sacrifice of Jesus on our behalf take our place before His Courts. As we do, these nations can see the reason for His birth and all His other activities become reality. There can be *peace of earth* because the government of God and its peace are increasing.

Not only do we see the rights of the devil revoked as we stand in the Courts of Heaven, we can petition the Lord for His purposes to be done. God promised us in Ezekiel 36:36-37 (NKJV) that He will give us the honor of standing before Him and making request based on His promises. This is what we do in the Courts of Heaven:

"Then the nations which are left all around you shall know that I, the Lord, have rebuilt the ruined places and planted what was desolate. I, the Lord, have spoken it, and I will do it." Thus says the Lord God: "I will also let the house of Israel inquire of Me to do this for them: I will increase their men like a flock."

God made very powerful promises to His people about their nation. Then He says, *"I will let them inquire of Me to do it."* God gives us the honor of being part of the process. We not only see any legal rights the devil is claiming revoked, we get to petition the Lord for His promises to be fulfilled.

This is again what God meant in Isaiah 43:26 when He said, *"Put Me in remembrance."* In other words, tell Me what I have promised You. When we do this, we are presenting our case before His Courts. We are asking and believing that God's Word is true. We are expressing before Him that all Jesus was born into the earth for will become a reality. Nations will be reclaimed for the glory of God. Judgment and justice are being established in divine order as the increase of His government and peace are come.

INVITATION

Jesus was born into the world to announce the arrival of the Kingdom of God. This Kingdom to this day is expanding through His saints standing in the Courts of Heaven. They are securing judgment and justice from these Courts. The end results will be His government of peace established in the nations. He is waiting for all His enemies to be put under His feet. We are the people assigned by Him to continue the process He began when He entered the earth two thousand years ago. May we step before the Courts of Heaven on behalf of His purposes in the nations. May we see His Kingdom come and His will be done on earth as it is in Heaven. Of the increase of His government and peace, there will be no end!

ROBERT HENDERSON is a global apostolic leader who operates in revelation and impartation. His teaching empowers the body of Christ to see the hidden truths of Scripture clearly and apply them for breakthrough results. Driven by a mandate to disciple nations through writing and speaking, Robert travels extensively around the globe, teaching on the apostolic, the Kingdom of God, the "Seven Mountains," and most notably, the Courts of Heaven. He and his wife, Mary, have been married for forty years. They have six children and five grandchildren. Together they are enjoying life in beautiful Waco, Texas.

KNOW THE
ONE YOU'RE
LOOKING FOR

by John Bevere

*A*dvent is defined as "the arrival of a notable person, thing, or event." For Christians worldwide, Advent is a season observed as a time of celebrating the birth of Jesus—His first coming—while also being mindful and expectant for His second coming.

When we consider the first coming of Jesus, He arrived in a way most were not expecting. The people of Israel were anxiously anticipating the manifestation of their promised Messiah. They were expectant as it was the season He was to appear. They were not unlike many Christians in our day, for most know we are in the time period preceding His second coming.

Jesus said we would know the season or generation, but not the day or hour. So, there is no reason to think it odd that the Israelites knew the season of His first coming. In fact, they had more to go on, as Daniel gave the timeframe in his prophetic writings (Daniel 9:24-26). The experts in the law were not surprised by the wise men of the East's inquiry and readily informed them where to find the child Jesus (see Matthew 2:4-5).

They knew the time was upon them—however, from their understanding of Old Testament Scripture, they formed an incorrect expectation of how their Messiah would come. Isaiah foretold, *"For unto us a Child is born, unto us a Son is given; and the government will be upon His shoulder. …Of the increase of His government and peace there will be no end, upon the throne of David and over His kingdom…from that time forward, even forever"* (Isaiah 9:6-7 NKJV).

The citizens of Israel were watching for a great King, one who would be both exceptionally wise and a powerful conqueror. This King would swiftly deliver them from Roman oppression and establish them as a nation without equal. He would reestablish the authority of the throne of David and would reign forever and ever. We see this in the fact that the scholars inquired of Jesus, *"When will God's kingdom realm come?"* (Luke 17:20-21 TPT). Not only the theologians, but the common people grappled with this as well. For most, the litmus test of Messiah's manifestation would be a king sitting on a physical throne in Jerusalem.

Can you imagine the conflict and confusion? When Jesus came as one of their own, raised in their schools, playing in their streets, building household furniture, and surrounded by tax collectors and prostitutes, they were blindsided.

CONFUSION

"Wait a minute!" they cried—feeling confused, "This isn't the way we expected the Messiah to come!"

Israel's leaders had more at stake. They anxiously awaited His coming, believing they would be made under-rulers of this new kingdom established in Jerusalem. So when Jesus came on the scene as a common man from Galilee, they disdained Him. He didn't fit the image of their Messiah either.

Let's fast-forward to after the resurrection. Even Jesus' own disciples, who now knew He was the Messiah, were still struggling with this conflict, "Okay, it's clear You are the Messiah, so when will the Kingdom the Scriptures speak of manifest? Why isn't it happening yet?" (see Acts 1:6).

Most didn't realize there would be a few thousand years between the statement *"a Son is given"* and the total realization and physical fulfillment, *"Of the increase of His government and peace there will be no end."*

This incident, along with others like it throughout the Scriptures, reveals a truth that is hard to grasp—God will often work in ways we cannot fathom! *Only those with eyes to see will discern His ways.*

Here's the clear reality—most were holding on to *an incorrect expectation* of the arrival of Messiah; watching for a mighty conquering Messiah as well, a hero who would deliver God's people from Roman oppression.

In contrast, let's look at another man who was also watching for the Messiah. His name is Simeon, of whom the Gospel of Luke records:

> *At that time there was a man in Jerusalem named Simeon. He was **righteous** and **devout** and was eagerly waiting for the Messiah to come and rescue Israel. The Holy Spirit was upon him and had revealed to him that he would not die until he had seen the Lord's Messiah. That day, the Spirit led him to the Temple. So when Mary and Joseph came to present the baby Jesus to the Lord as the law required, Simeon was there. He took the child in his arms and praised God…* (Luke 2:25–28 NLT).

While Simeon held Jesus in his arms, he spoke a prophetic declaration over this one-month-old baby—acknowledging Him as the Messiah. This is where it becomes interesting! Here is a man who recognizes the Messiah when He is but thirty days old—yet all of

Nazareth, the Pharisees, and the majority in the nation still couldn't recognize Jesus as Messiah when He is in His thirties—performing signs and wonders no human before Him ever accomplished!

So what was the difference? It was *the ability to see through spiritual discernment.* This was the difference between Simeon and the others. With this in mind, the question remains—how did Simeon develop the ability to see and discern spiritually?

RIGHTEOUS AND DEVOUT

To find our answer, let's return to the account of Simeon in Luke 2:25-28. There we discover two specific character traits that distinguish him—he was *righteous* and *devout.* First, I want to focus on the word *devout.* The Greek meaning for this word is defined as "pertaining to being reverent toward God; pious." With this understanding, we can say that Simeon was righteous and reverentially feared the Lord.

The fear of the Lord is the foundation to knowing God intimately. Solomon—known as the wisest man who ever lived—penned, *"The fear of the Lord is the beginning of knowledge"* (Proverbs 1:7 NKJV). The following chapter in Proverbs clarifies the type of knowledge Solomon is referring to. He states that by the fear of the Lord we will gain the knowledge of God (Proverbs 2:1-5). To put it in terms we are more familiar with—it means you will come to know God intimately.

Holy fear is what separates those who know God superficially from those who walk closely with Him. An intimate relationship with God will not even begin until the fear of the Lord is first established in our hearts. This is the most rewarding facet of walking in the fear of the Lord and it's the reason we see the Holy Spirit coming upon Simeon, leading him into the temple, and empowering him to discern the Messiah while He was an infant.

David—a man who pursued the heart of God—also understood the reward of holy fear. He wrote, *"The secret of the Lord is with those who fear Him..."* (Psalm 25:14 NKJV). Do we share secrets with acquaintances or intimate friends? Yes, with those who are closest to us. God in essence is saying, "My intimate, close friends are those who fear Me." The NLT version amplifies this by translating the verse, *"The Lord is a friend to those who fear him."* God is close with those who fear Him. This fear is not to be afraid of God; rather, it is to be terrified to be distant from Him. These lovers of God separate themselves from anything and everything that would come between them and the Lord. Those who are afraid of God run away from Him, but those who reverentially fear Him run *to* Him. His presence is both their delight and their hiding place. This close proximity results in intimacy.

The other aspect about Simeon that separated him from the others is that he was *righteous*. Simeon lived a godly lifestyle that pleased God. This was the evidence of his reverential fear of the Lord. Paul, writing to the church in Corinth, states, *"...Beloved, let us cleanse ourselves from all filthiness of the flesh and spirit, perfecting holiness in the fear of God"* (2 Corinthians 7:1 NKJV).

HOLINESS

A life of holiness is produced and made mature by the fear of the Lord. When we fear God, we obey Him—we love what He loves and hate what He hates. We delight in God's Word as we esteem His commands above our own desires. Solomon verifies this truth: *"...By the fear of the Lord one departs from evil"* (Proverbs 16:6 NKJV).

Because holiness has been communicated incorrectly in the past, many have shunned it all together—associating it with llegalism, bondage, and mean-spirited preachers. Yet, New Testament holiness is not even remotely connected to works of the law or legalism. It's actually a life-giving and beautiful way of life that is greatly misunderstood.

One of the core definitions of holiness is to be set apart. It can be compared to a bride who sets herself apart exclusively for her husband. As she prioritizes her covenant to her husband, she cuts ties with her former lovers and gives herself completely to her bridegroom. This is why the Bible empathically states: *"Pursue...holiness, without which no one will see the Lord"* (Hebrews 12:14 NKJV). If holiness positions us to see the Lord, then why would any child of God avoid discussing it? If that is the case, then holiness should be the talk of the town! With this in mind, let's take a look at what Jesus promised:

A little while longer and the world will see Me no more,
but you will see Me. Because I live, you will live also.
…He who has My commandments and keeps them, it is
he who loves Me. And he who loves Me will be loved by
My Father, and I will love him and manifest Myself to
him (John 14:19,21 NKJV).

There are two important facts that must not be
ignored. First, a very real component of Christianity is
seeing Jesus. Why is seeing Jesus important? Because
if we don't see Him, we can't know Him—we can only
know about Him. This can be likened to those who know
a lot about celebrities yet have never actually known
them in a personal way. They may know all the latest
rumors and gossip—yet lack a personal relationship with
them. This is where the Pharisees missed the mark—they
knew about God, yet could not recognize the Son of God
standing in their midst.

Second, those who obey the Lord and keep His
commandments will experience a level of intimacy that
cannot be known any other way. Jesus pointed out that
only those who keep His commandments are the ones
to whom He will make Himself known. They will be the
ones who see Him, who enter His presence, and thereby
come to know Him intimately. *This privilege is not promised*
to all believers, only to those—who like Simeon—are devout and
live righteously.

Solomon lived a life in which he experienced both
success and failure. He had everything this world could
offer—fame, power, riches, status—you name it, he had

it. However, he lost his fear of God and it manifested in him disobeying God in marrying multiple wives who had no relationship with God. The book of Ecclesiastes is a picture of a man who is disillusioned and cynical. Yet, thankfully Solomon regained his right mind and in the end writes this conclusion to life: *"That's the whole story. Here now is my final conclusion: Fear God and obey his commands, for this is everyone's duty"* (Ecclesiastes 12:13 NLT).

NOT CAUGHT BY SURPRISE

Let's return now to the main focus of this discussion—no one knows the day or the hour in which the Lord Jesus will return, but almost all of us are aware that it's the season. However, those who embrace the fear of the Lord will not be caught by surprise or have errant expectations of His manifestation. Paul says it like this, *"But you aren't in the dark about these things, dear brothers and sisters, and you won't be surprised when the day of the Lord comes like a thief"* (1 Thessalonians 5:4 NLT).

When we live a life that is both righteous and devout, not only will we be discerning—we'll also be ready for the advent of the Lord's second coming. In regard to our time, Peter warned:

> *But the day of the Lord will come as a thief in the night, in which the heavens will pass away with a great noise, and the elements will melt with fervent heat; both the earth and the works that are in it will be burned up. Therefore, since all these things will be dissolved, **what***

manner of persons ought you to be in holy conduct and godliness, looking for and hastening the coming of the day of God… (2 Peter 3:10-12 NKJV).

INVITATION

The return of our King will come unannounced, like a thief. **In the meantime, choosing a life of holiness in which we set ourselves apart to God will ensure we remain close to Him and know the One we're looking for.** *Furthermore, as we live holy—not only will we remain close to our Lord—we'll "hasten" His coming. To "hasten" means to quicken. It's to cause something to happen sooner than it otherwise would. As the Lord observes His bride preparing herself for Him—it fuels His desire to bring her to Himself.*

Friend, be encouraged, for soon and very soon, the One who is appearing will come without delay. Let's live holy and ready for the Lord's appearing.

JOHN BEVERE and his wife, **LISA**, are the founders of Messenger International. A minister and best-selling author, John delivers messages of uncompromising truth with boldness and passion. His desire is to support the local church and resource leaders regardless of location, language, or financial position. To this end, his resources have been translated into more than one hundred languages, and millions of copies have been given to pastors and leaders worldwide. When he's home, John tries to convince Lisa to take up golf and spends time with his four sons, daughters-in-law, and grandbabies.

THE GLORY HAS COME

Christmas has come—and gone. The gift wrap has been thrown away, the tree is on the side of the road awaiting the garbage truck—or stored in the attic, if you're like my family—the relatives have returned to their respective locations, and we get ready to venture into a new year. A new season.

And shockingly, soon enough, we find ourselves preparing to engage the season all over again.

I pray that the power of what we call Christmas would live in your heart all year long. Don't wait for December to roll around to study and engage with what we know as the "Christmas story." After reading the different entries and writing a few myself, I am convinced this season carries prophetic blueprints on how we are called to host a move of God in our lives, and on earth. True, there was no greater move of God than the Incarnation—God leaving His throne, becoming a seed, supernaturally deposited into the womb of a teenager, and being birthed into the humblest of conditions.

Yet, that move of God, Heaven to earth, throne to animal feeding trough, reveals something about *where* glory comes and who are the first people to behold it. Glory is attracted to the humble and lowly. Glory is discovered by shepherds. Glory is displayed among animals and peasants. Glory in the highest is actually experienced by those willing to go the lowest. After all, *He did.*

What does it mean to "Go low" to find and encounter His glory? It doesn't refer to an economic or social status, as the affluent magi (wise men), sought out the Messiah's presence at potential risk to their lives from King Herod. Going low is a posture of the heart. It means surrendering to the ways of God that are higher than ours and the thoughts of God that are far beyond our own (see Isaiah 55:8-9).

Going low means saying yes to impossible assignments and seemingly foolish tasks—for example, a teenage virgin girl receiving a mandate from archangel Gabriel to carry the Messiah in her womb. It means being willing to look for the movement of the Royal King in some of the darkest, most hostile environments among some of the most unlikely and unexpected people.

Simply put, let's not bind God to fulfill our expectations. Let's not imprison Him according to our traditions and ideas of what He should do, or how He should move. He seeks those with hearts with room to receive their King. There was no room at the inn, true. But may there be room in our hearts to receive Him, at Christmas and always.

ABOUT THE AUTHOR

LARRY SPARKS is publisher for Destiny Image, a Spirit-filled publishing house birthed in 1983 with a mandate to publish the prophets. With a MDiv. in Church History and Renewal from Regent University, Larry is a prophetic minister who teaches individuals and church environments how to create space for the Holy Spirit to move in presence, prophetic utterance and power. Larry has been featured on Sid Roth's *It's Supernatural!*, *The Jim Bakker Show*, CBN, TBN, the Elijahlist, and *Charisma* magazine. Larry is also host of *The Prophetic Edge* featured on GOD TV. He lives in Texas with his wife and daughter. For more information visit: larrysparksministries.com.